PIZZA

COOKERY

PIZZA
COOKERY

●

CEIL DYER

●

MC GRAW-HILL BOOK COMPANY
New York   St. Louis   San Francisco
Toronto   Hamburg   Mexico

1 2 3 4 5 6 7 8 9 0 DOCDOC 8 9 8 7 6 5 4

ISBN 0-07-018542-5{HC}
ISBN 0-07-018543-3{PBK.}

LIBRARY OF CONGRESS CATALOGING IN PUBLICATION DATA

Dyer, Ceil.
Pizza cookery.
Includes index.
1. Pizza. I. Title.
TX770.D9 1983   641.8′24   83-11306
ISBN 0-07-018542-5
ISBN 0-07-018543-3 (pbk.)

Book design by Iris Weinstein

Contents

1

An Introduction to Pizza Making

EVERYBODY LOVES PIZZA!

This is a book on how to prepare pizza, all types of pizza.

Pizza has become as popular in this country as hamburgers and hot dogs. We all love it. We buy it from fast food stores, we buy it frozen and we buy it ready to bake from a mix. But we seldom make it at home from "scratch," because, until now, there were very few recipes available. Yet pizza making is fun and easy. Pizza's quick to make and can be prepared ahead of time. It's perfect for parties. Pizza can be a meal or a snack or a dessert. You can even have pizza for breakfast.

Parents complain that their children would rather go out for pizza then stay home for an "old-fashioned meal." You can't blame them. Pizza tastes good. It's exciting. It has great flavor "plus." Why not give them what they want? A homemade pizza made with fresh vegetables, fine cheese and good meat can be as nourishing as a meal of meat, potatoes and vegetables. It's just more fun to eat.

Appetizer pizzas are sensational. At cocktail parties, the crudités remain on the table, while the pizza goes like frost on a windowpane when the sun comes up.

And when it comes to dessert pizzas, well, they are the most exciting and newest "sweet ending" in town. They look positively beautiful, and they taste grand.

The only difficulty in making pizza is to prepare enough, but that becomes a very easy task when you have the right directions. In fact it's as easy as pie, or easier, really.

When we started testing recipes for this book, we were surprised, really surprised, by how many and what a variety of people wanted to help: a young football player who wanted to learn because he "just loved pizza"; an elegantly thin career girl who didn't like to cook but thought pizza making would be fun; a young couple into health food who wanted to use only fresh ingredients; a bachelor who wanted to serve pizza to his girl friend; and a variety of other people who hadn't realized pizza was more "in" these days then French *haute cuisine.* It all goes to show that just about everyone likes pizza—especially when it's homemade.

But why make pizza when it can be had from a takeout shop a few minutes away? Simply because it's more fun, more satisfying, more pleasurable to make your own exciting pizza creation than it is to buy an assembly-line product. Besides, homemade pizza has much more pizazz.

Home pizza makers can take advantage of a wide variety of different foodstuffs: extra virgin olive oil, vine-ripened tomatoes, fresh basil and other herbs, fine imported ham and many different kinds of sausage ranging from sweet to hot. And, in addition to the usual grated Romano, Parmesan and mozzarella, any number of other equally delicious cheeses can add new dimensions to pizza.

If that's not enough, you don't have to limit yourself to thinking Italian. Possibilities for pizza toppings are endless. Serve a French-style pizza with fresh tomato sauce and blue cheese as an appetizer—your guests will love it. Present a Mexican pizza to a teenage gathering. Make a pizza with an eggplant topping or let eggplant substitute for pizza dough crust—it's low in calories and tastes terrific. In the pages that follow you'll find recipes for these pizzas, which can't help but please you, your friends and family. But do try all of the other pizzas described here as well. We guarantee you will like every one. Not just the eating, but the baking and serving, too.

AN UNAUTHORIZED HISTORY OF PIZZA

One day an Italian housewife was gazing out her kitchen window while pondering what to do with her excess bread dough. Just then a handsome young farmer carrying a large basket of fresh, ripe tomatoes came by the window.

"What wonderful tomatoes!" she thought to herself. Suddenly the young man tripped over a stone and fell, crushing his basket of tomatoes. The concerned housewife rushed to his aid, and in a flash of genius realized exactly what she could do with *her* dough and *his* tomatoes! This bit of history was sent to us by the Sassafras Company along with our Great Big Chicago-Style Pizza Pan. True? Well, we are not sure, but it just could be.

While researching the origin of pizza, we came across a disturbing fact: it seems there are as many theories about pizza's invention as there are ethnic groups who claim to have discovered this country.

For instance, several old books on Italian cookery trace pizza's beginning to a Sicilian baker who topped it with only garlic and oil. Tomatoes and herbs soon followed, but it was not until 1889 that cheese was added, to a pizza created expressly for a pizza-loving Italian princess named Margherita.

It is reported that the first pizzeria in America was opened in the early 1900s. It specialized in Pizza Margherita, which they renamed Pizza Neapolitan Style: thin crust, round shape, deliciously topped with tomato, cheese and sometimes sausage.

Although this restaurant catered primarily to Italian immigrants who lived in Manhattan's "Little Italy," its fame soon spread. In no time at all there were dozens of pizza restaurants, not just in New York, but in every one of our states. Now, pizza is as familiar to Americans as hamburgers, and just as popular.

These days you can have pizza Neapolitan, Sicilian, New York, Chicago or California style: topped not just with traditional Italian tomato sauce and cheese, but with almost anything that appeals to your taste.

INGREDIENTS

There are certain tastes and aromas that, once experienced, remain in your memory. The astonishing intensity of a truly great Italian pizza combined with the rich bouquet of a classic Chianti wine add up to something you simply cannot forget. Nothing can quite measure up to that first slice, that first sip, of the best.

What makes a fine Neapolitan or Sicilian pizza such a work of art? Not even in Italy can you obtain a precise recipe. Although pizza has long been considered one of the greatest of all Italian culinary creations, it seems no two pizza makers can agree on what combination of ingredients is essential to its total success.

Nonetheless, as with all fine cookery, great pizza making starts at the marketplace—with the selection of the finest ingredients available.

● PIZZA CRUST

Let's begin with the basics: the yeast, flour and oil you will need for your pizza crust dough.

The way you mix, knead, let rise and shape the dough will affect the final result, of course, but your crust's texture and taste will be no better than the ingredients that go into it.

PIZZA FLOUR

Although you can make a perfectly acceptable dough for pizza with bleached, enriched, all-purpose flour, the unbleached variety produces better results. Of all the American brands we tested, we found Ceresota (sometimes labeled Heckers brand) to be the best blend of hard and soft wheat, closest to professional baker's flour and very similar in performance to semolina (hard durum wheat flour), the flour used in Italy for all pizza making.

As for semolina itself, we love it. It produces a bouncy, light, easy-to-handle dough, and a crust with a superb texture and taste: chewy yet crisp, but not dry, with a flavor rather like San Francisco sourdough bread.

Although semolina for pizza and other Italian baking is not generally available, it can be found in Italian grocery shops or ordered by mail (see the Appendix). Don't confuse this finely ground product with the coarsely ground pasta semolina you will find in numerous gourmet shops; although a small amount of this can be added to all-purpose flour for flavor, it is too coarse to use alone, except in pasta making.

THE BEST OIL FOR PIZZA

Pizza dough requires fine olive oil. The finest is not necessarily the most expensive, but the freshest you can find. Fresh olive oil does not have a strong, assertive aroma, but a pleasurable, delicate fragrance vaguely reminiscent of the olive itself. It need not be imported from Italy; some of the fruitiest and best

5

oils come not only from Sicily, Spain and Greece, but now also in limited quantities from California in the U.S. of A.

To get the freshest olive oil, find a store where it is extremely popular, frequently sold. Once opened, the oil should be kept refrigerated. Contrary to some opinions, olive oil becomes rancid if left at room temperature for more than a short time.

YEAST

Although we definitely like the double yeasty flavor of fresh yeast and use it when we can find it, more often than not we find that it is well past its prime. For this reason, we recommend using individual, dated packages of dry yeast. It is much more reliable and therefore preferable for most home baking. (One package of dry yeast is equivalent to one ounce of fresh yeast.)

● SAUCES AND TOPPINGS

Now for what covers the crust of any great pizza: here is the fun part of pizza making and the best possible reason for making your own.

TOMATOES

Not just any tomato will do for a great pizza. Fresh, vine-ripened plum tomatoes are our first choice for a classic Pizza Margherita (Pizza Neapolitan Style), but only when they can be obtained at their peak of perfection—and preferably from your own garden. When these are not available, we opt for imported Italian plum tomatoes: inside the can you should find them to be deep red, firm and whole, proving they are handpicked and ripened naturally. We prefer this type of tomato for making our own pizza sauce, too. When teamed with just the right blend of herbs and other good things, they make a covering for pizza crust that is truly magnificent, worthy of the toppings to follow.

HERBS FOR PIZZA PERFECTION

Italy's favorite herbs are the ingredients that transform plain tomato sauce into a seductive topping for pizza. You can't prepare a great pizza without them. It is impossible to describe these herbs adequately—you must experience their persuasive aromas and flavors for yourself. Though you may use other seasonings as well, these are the herbs that make pizza, pizza. Note that we've listed them, not alphabetically, but in order of their importance.

Oregano. We have been told that the sale of oregano in this country has more than quadrupled in the past few years. This must be due, at least in good part, to the increasing popularity of pizza. This herb, an elegant, leafy perennial, complements almost any tomato dish. It is robust and assertive, reminiscent of the savory dishes of Mediterranean cookery.

Basil. If we could have only one herb in our garden, it would be basil. It is one of the most delicate and aromatic of all herbs. Easy to grow in your own garden, or in a clay pot on a sunny windowsill, basil imparts the rich, warm fragrance of summer itself. Dried basil can be substituted for fresh, of course; though it is not as potent, it is preferable to no basil at all. (To bring out the flavor of dried basil, soak it beforehand in a little wine or vermouth, or add it to the olive oil you will use to sauté ingredients such as onions and garlic.)

Rosemary. The character of this fragrant plant was captured well in 1759 by one William Langham, who wrote, "Rosemary is lively, joyful, liking and youngly." Sweetly persuasive, for some rosemary symbolizes remembrance; and remember it you will in any cookery, especially when added to pizza sauce.

Marjoram. Marjoram was cultivated by the Greeks, who believed that Aphrodite had created it and named it "joy of the mountain." Doesn't that sound grand? One enthusiastic writer states that marjoram should be used in all dishes. Perhaps not, but certainly it should be used in pizza cookery. It adds an incomparable depth of flavor.

● THE WONDERFUL WORLD OF CHEESES FOR PIZZA

Mozzarella. There are several kinds. Skim-milk mozzarella is the cheese most often associated with American pizza. It melts into long, satiny strands that are part of the fun of pizza eating. Whole-milk mozzarella is richer and has a fuller flavor. Although it melts to a smooth, creamy texture, it is not quite so stringy. Buffalo-milk mozzarella is often the gourmet's choice. This variety tastes as rich as its price—so much so that we prefer it in small quantities combined with American skim-milk mozzarella.

Parmesan. True Parmesan cheese is made only in Italy, with the same care and expertise found in the production of fine wine in France. Made from milk produced between the first of April and the middle of November in the provinces of Parma, Reggio, Modena and Bologna, this cheese is aged at least 18 months before it is brought to market. Straw-yellow in color with a crumbly but moist texture, it tastes mellow, yet slightly sharp and a little bit salty. To buy the real thing, look for the words "Parmigiano-Reggiano" printed in small dots in a constantly repeated pattern over the entire surface of the crust. Without these markings, it is not true Parmesan. This is not to say that other cheeses labeled Parmesan are not to be used; we have found excellent alternatives, at much lower prices and with very similar consistency, imported from many other parts of the world. For best quality, however, Parmesan cheese should be purchased in one piece from a fine cheese shop and grated at home as used, not purchased pre-grated from your supermarket in small paper cylinders. Though such pre-grated cheeses need not be totally ignored, they do not have the true flavor, texture or taste of "the real thing."

Romano. Although Romano is often suggested as an alternative to Parmesan cheese, it is much sharper and more powerful. Its aggressive taste gives an added robust quality when sprinkled over the top of your pizza.

Fontina. This pale-yellow, smooth, semi-soft cheese has a delicate, sweet, nut-like flavor that melts to a smooth covering.

Bel Paese. Another Italian creation that is often duplicated in this country, at its best Bel Paese is creamy, soft and buttery. However, it can be mild to strong in flavor depending on where and how it is made.

Provolone. Imported Italian provolone is sharp and smoky, and its earthy pungency becomes more pronounced with age. American cheeses by this name bear only a slight resemblance to the Italian original.

Ricotta. This cheese is a by-product of other cheeses, made from whey, a watery milk residue. Ricotta has a rich, fresh, slightly tart taste that blends well with any number of other ingredients to make a grand filling for calzones, double-crust pie-pan pizzas and sweet pizza desserts.

Other cheeses we have used with great success as pizza toppings include mild-yet-tangy blue, mellow Swiss, smooth Monterey Jack and elegant Port du Salut. These are only a few of the many, however. Any cheese of good quality that melts to a smooth, creamy texture can be used for excitingly different varieties of pizza.

● SOME OF THE MANY SAUSAGES AND HAMS TO GLORIFY PIZZA

There are so many different kinds of sausage, ham and other cured meat you can use for pizza enhancement that we can give you only a small part of the list.

Pepperoni. This highly seasoned sausage is the one most often used as a pizza topping. Made of beef and pork with lots of fiery red pepper, black pepper and garlic, it is a powerhouse of flavor.

Italian salami. The Italian version of this familiar sausage is a combination of chopped pork and beef, often mixed with red wine and highly seasoned with garlic and spices. Magnificent.

Mortadella. We sometimes think this is the best-tasting sausage you can buy. A bologna with a smooth, subtle flavoring, mortadella is made of finely chopped pork and beef, larded with pork fat, then smoked and dried.

Sicilian salami. This spicy, flavorful salami is made entirely of ground pork flavored with both white and black pepper.

Soppressata. Chunky, coarsely ground pork studded with peppercorns and made pungent with other spices.

Calabrese. Hot peppers add fiery flavor to this coarsely ground salami.

Capicollo. Another spicy and extremely likeable hot sausage made with pork that is cured and air-dried.

Italian-style link sausage. This uncooked sausage can be either mild and sweet, or spicy and hot, and is usually

10

flavored with fennel and/or other herbs. It can be just good or truly great in flavor depending on where and how it is made.

Prosciutto. Although Italian prosciutto cannot now be imported into this country, you will find a number of excellent American-made brands produced in exactly the same way— salted and air-cured. It's expensive but extremely flavorful, so a small amount will go a long way. If you can't find it in your area, you can substitute (although it *will* be a substitute) Smithfield ham or any other smoked or dry-cured ham.

Pancetta. Pancetta is Italian-style bacon; however, it is not smoked, but salt-cured, lightly spiced and rolled into a cylinder shape. Like prosciutto it can be eaten "out of hand," but it may also be fried or used in place of American bacon in any dish.

● OLIVES THAT BRING PIZZA TO LIFE

We love to use a number of different olives, from mild to pungent and sharp, for our pizzas. Their saltiness and earthy flavors seem to make a pizza complete. These are our favorites.

Niçoise. This small, almond-shaped olive is a must for Mediterranean cookery. It is cured in brine, then packed in oil. Frequently, herbs of Provence are added to give an extra dimension of flavor.

Sicilian. An alternative to the purply-black olives found on most pizzas. These are green olives, cracked to absorb the salty brine in which they are cured, and spiced with oregano and red pepper.

Kalamata. These jumbo-sized, blue-black Greek olives add maximum flavor and are often considered the best of all the great imported varieties of olives.

Royal (or *Victoria*). Black olives from Greece, cured in olive oil, these have a wonderfully soft texture and mild taste.

Gaeta. Satiny smooth, small midnight-black olives packed in brine or in oil and herbs.

Greek black. Blue-black, meaty and brine-cured, with a pungent "have another" flavor. These are the olives you'll most often find sold in bulk in gourmet shops and top-quality delicatessens.

Alfonso. Big, black, delicate and flavorful. One of America's best adaptations of an Italian specialty.

PIZZA EQUIPMENT

You don't need special equipment to make pizza. A pizza can be baked in a jelly roll pan or on a long, flat baking sheet. For a traditional large, round, flat pizza, however, you will want a pizza pan, 12 or 14 inches in diameter. When you become as enthusiastic about making and serving pizzas as you are about eating them, you may very well want to add a baking stone and baker's peel. Both add a professional pizza maker's touch to your kitchen.

Before baking stones were generally available, many cookbook authors recommended lining your oven with unglazed 6-inch quarry tiles to transform your home oven into something like the old-fashioned brick ovens still used by many fine, professional bakers. However, a baking stone is made of one large slab instead of several small squares, and performs the same function, so it is much more satisfactory. Made of heavy, refractory material, it retains intense heat, absorbs moisture, and gives your pizza an evenly browned, very crisp bottom crust. It also comes with a metal rack which makes removing your baked pizza from the hot oven easier. (If your baking stone does not come with a rack, you can purchase one separately.)

You'll find baking stones in both round and oblong shapes. The round one is perfect for a traditional pizza; however, you may also want to own an oblong stone—for preparing several small pizzas, or for calzones. The baking stone must always be put in place when the oven is turned on and preheated before the pizza is added.

A baker's peel is a large, flat, wooden disk with a beveled edge and a short handle. You'll need it (or a reasonable facsimile) to slide your prepared pizza onto the hot baking stone.

With the exception of a pizza cutting wheel, which is fun to use but not essential (a serrated knife is equally efficient), undoubtedly you already have all of the other equipment you'll need for pizza preparation. Nonetheless, to serve as a reminder, here is the list:

A large bowl and a heavy spoon, or an electric food processor, for mixing dough

A flat work surface sufficiently large for kneading and shaping dough

A bowl large enough to hold the dough as it rises to double in bulk

Sharp knives for mincing and chopping vegetables and toppings

A hand grater, or an electric food processor, for grinding and shredding cheeses

Large, heavy skillets and saucepans for pre-cooking vegetables and making sauces

Plus, and perhaps most important of all, your own efficient hands, your sharp eyes and your good taste. No great cooking can be accomplished without them.

ENTERTAINING WITH PIZZA

What makes a great party? Any party should, of course, be suited to the season, the location and the mood of the moment, but the basics are always the same: pleasurable surroundings plus great food and drink presented in an appetizing, harmonious way.

Preparation for a party should be pleasurable, too. Nothing can spoil your party more thoroughly than overwork on your part. Simplicity is the key, especially if you are making all the preparations alone.

Pizza is the ideal party fare, either as an appetizer or as the star of the meal. Pizza is fun to make, it looks great, and we've yet to find anyone who does not find it utterly delicious. Design your menu around pizza, and give your creativity free rein! Then your party will be the success it should be—a pleasurable, relaxed and happy time you give with affection to your friends.

We've composed three basic menus for the recipes in this book and list them here as a guide. We think you will find them useful in themselves, but they are also meant to inspire you to create your own combinations. The first menu is for a conventional dinner, the second for an informal buffet, and the third for entertaining a crowd.

PIZZA MENUS

CONVENTIONAL DINNER PARTY

*PISSALADIERE** or RIVIERA-STYLE PIZZA*
to serve with before-dinner drinks
Sautéed veal scallops or broiled chicken
A crisp-cooked fresh vegetable
Chilled white wine, or mellow room-temperature red wine
GRANITA DI CAFFÈ* or SHERBET SURPRISE*

BUFFET SUPPER

DEEP-DISH CHICAGO-STYLE PIZZA* or
SICILIAN PIZZA*
ITALIAN SALAD WITH MARINATED ARTICHOKE HEARTS*
CRISP-COOKED VEGETABLE SALAD WITH
MUSTARD VINAIGRETTE*
Pineapple sticks, honeydew melon balls, cantaloupe
slices, orange sections and grapes
Icy cold pale ale or chianti
Imported Italian Chocolates
Coffee

BIG BASH

A SEAFOOD BAR:
Cold boiled shrimp and scallops, oysters and clams
on the half shell
arranged on large trays of crushed ice
Cocktail sauce and horseradish dip
A VARIETY OF PIZZAS
set out on one long table so that everyone can sample at least two
BEAUTIFUL UGLI FRUIT AND AVOCADO SALAD*
Belgium endive, romaine hearts and bibb lettuce
in a big salad bowl with clear French dressing
on a separate table across the room
APRICOT PIZZA FLAMBÉ*
Coffee
Champagne, chilled white wine, Italian red wine, and icy cold beer
* indicates recipe found in this book

2

In the Beginning: Pizza Breads

FOCACCIA (PIZZA BREAD)

This chewy, fine-grained Italian peasant bread is not only the fastest yeast bread you can make but also the most satisfying. The dough—which is the same as the dough used for pizza crust—is easy to prepare, and the result is truly delicious: a round, puffy loaf with a crisp, light, golden crust, tender but firm throughout. This is a bread to enjoy all the way through. You can serve *focaccia* as a table bread; as a snack with anything from coffee, tea or cold milk to fine wine or even champagne; or, if you fill it with a savory stuffing, as the star of a light luncheon or late evening meal, in place of a sandwich.

Focaccia (from the Latin word *focus*, meaning "hearth") is directly descended from the earliest type of bread ever made. It was first baked on a flat stone on an open hearth, under a cover of hot ashes from the fire. When the cook declared it done (and this was learned only after many mistakes and long experience) the ashes were brushed off and the loaf taken from the heat. In time, the open hearth was replaced by a brick oven and the bread baked directly on the bricks, as it is still done in many parts of Italy. Although today *focaccia* is more often made at a professional bakery, the recipe remains essentially the same.

Making this bread is so uncomplicated that you'll soon find the written recipe almost unnecessary. At first, though, it may help you to follow these simple guidelines:

- Remember to bring all of the ingredients to room temperature before you begin. If you keep your oil in the refrigerator, as you should, this is one ingredient you are apt to forget.
- Remember that yeast is a living organism and is affected by temperature. It should be dissolved in lukewarm water. Hot water will destroy it, and cold water will not allow it to activate. Ideally, water temperature should be from 105° to 110° F, but you can learn to

gauge warmth by pouring a little over the back of your wrist; it should feel just comfortably warm.

- Exactly how much flour and water you will need to make a perfect dough depends very much on the type and brand of flour used. For instance, semolina (durum wheat flour) requires less water than does unbleached white flour. When you follow the basic recipes here, add water or flour as needed to make a soft but not sticky dough that can be turned out and kneaded with only a little more flour until it becomes quite springy, very smooth and elastic.

- The rising time is very short for this type of bread. If you are not ready to bake it once it has doubled in volume, you can punch it down and let it rise a second time before it is shaped and baked.

- Remember to preheat your oven at least 15 to 20 minutes before baking your loaf.

- Don't overbake your *focaccia*. Baking time can vary slightly, so when your loaf has been in the oven for about 30 minutes and looks big and golden brown, take it out. Then, using a clean dish towel to protect your hands, turn it over and tap it lightly on the bottom. If it sounds hollow, it is done.

- It's a real temptation to slice and eat this bread as soon as it comes out of the oven. However, if you wait 5 to 10 minutes, it will taste even better, slice more evenly, yet still be fragrant and warm.

INFORMAL KITCHEN BUFFET

A tureen of homemade soup, fish chowder or
oyster stew

PIZZA BREAD* stuffed with a savory filling

A straw basket of purple and green grapes

Assorted little cakes

Coffee

● BASIC PIZZA BREAD

This dough makes a delicious loaf "as is," but it's also incredibly versatile. You can add herbs to your taste; stir bits of prosciutto or Genoa salami into the batter; transform it with a topping of onions or garlic; or fill it with a variety of delicious ingredients.

1 cup warm water (105° to 110° F)
1 teaspoon sugar
1 teaspoon salt
1 package dry yeast
1½ cups semolina (durum wheat flour) or all-purpose unbleached flour
3 tablespoons olive oil
⅛ teaspoon any of the following herbs: basil, rosemary, oregano, marjoram, sage (optional)

1 to 2 oz. prosciutto, Genoa salami or pepperoni, cut into thin slivers or finely diced (optional)
1 cup additional flour
Additional water, as needed
Additional flour, as needed

In a large bowl, combine water, sugar, salt and yeast. Stir once, then let stand until mixture is bubbly. Stir in 1½ cups semolina or all-purpose flour. Add oil and beat to a smooth batter. If desired, stir in herbs or add slivered or diced meat. Fold in the additional cup of flour to form a soft dough that will pull away from sides of bowl. If dough is too dry, sprinkle with a little water; if too sticky, knead in a little additional flour. Turn out on a lightly floured work surface and let stand while you wash, dry and lightly oil the bowl.

Sprinkle top of dough with a little more flour and begin kneading it, adding more flour as needed to keep it from sticking to your hands or the work surface. After about 8 minutes the dough will be smooth and elastic. When it can be bounced easily on the flour-free work surface, form it into a ball, place it in the oiled bowl and turn to coat all sides. Cover bowl with plastic wrap or a clean dish towel and set aside in a warm, draft-free place for 1½ to 2 hours, until dough has almost tripled in volume.

Punch dough down, then turn it out on a lightly floured work surface. Knead 3 to 4 minutes, then form again into a ball and let stand about 30 minutes.

If you are going to bake the loaf on a preheated baking stone, place the stone on center rack in oven. Preheat oven to 400° F.

Place dough on an inverted 12″ to 14″ pizza pan, a baking sheet or baker's peel. Press out into a circle 10″ to 11″ in diameter. Slide the loaf from the baker's peel onto the pre-heated stone, or place pan or baking sheet on center rack of oven. Bake for 25 to 30 minutes, or until crust is lightly browned.

Makes one 10″ to 11″ round loaf.

PIZZA BREAD WITH COARSE SALT

Basic Pizza Bread dough
1 teaspoon olive oil
1 teaspoon coarse (kosher) salt

Prepare Basic Pizza Bread dough. Just before baking, spread surface of dough evenly with oil and sprinkle with salt. Bake as directed.

PIZZA ONION BREAD

1 small onion, peeled and
  thinly sliced, slices broken
  into rings
1 tablespoon olive oil
1 teaspoon butter
Basic Pizza Bread dough

In a small skillet, sauté onion rings in oil and butter until very soft and pale golden. Set aside. Prepare Basic Pizza Bread dough. Just before baking, remove onions from oil with a slotted spoon and spread them evenly over the loaf, pressing them lightly into the dough. Spoon any oil and butter mixture remaining in the pan over the onions. Bake as directed.

PIZZA BREAD WITH GARLIC

2 cloves garlic, peeled, minced   1 teaspoon butter
1 teaspoon olive oil   Basic Pizza Bread dough

In a small skillet, cook garlic in butter and oil until soft and fragrant. Set aside. Prepare Basic Pizza Bread dough. Just before baking, spoon garlic and oil-butter mixture over top of loaf. Bake as directed.

PIZZA BREAD WITH CHEESE FILLING
We like to bake this filled loaf late in the day to serve still warm with dinner; in midsummer with a great big, beautiful salad; or after a blustery cold winter day as an accompaniment to a hearty minestrone.

Basic Pizza Bread dough   ½ teaspoon dried oregano
¼ lb. Monterey Jack cheese,   ¼ teaspoon dried basil
  coarsely chopped   1½ tablespoons olive oil
¼ lb. fontina cheese, coarsely   Water
  chopped
¼ lb. provolone cheese, coarsely
  chopped

Prepare Basic Pizza Bread dough and set aside to rise.

In a bowl, combine cheeses, oregano, basil and olive oil. Stir to blend. Set aside at room temperature until ready to use.

Preheat oven to 400° F.

When dough has risen, punch down and turn out on a lightly floured board. With floured hands, press it out into an 8″ x 6″ rectangle.

Cover lightly with a clean dish towel and let rest about 20 minutes. Then press out into a 16″ x 12″ rectangle. Place on long, flat baking sheet.

Drain oil from cheeses and set oil aside. Spread the cheeses in a 4″ band down the center of dough. Drizzle with a little of the reserved olive oil.

Fold the two short ends of the dough up and over the

21

filling. Moisten the long ends of the dough with a little water and pull up to completely enclose the filling, overlapping by about 1″ on top; press gently to seal. With a small, sharp knife slash top in several places to allow steam to escape. Let stand about 30 minutes.

Bake in preheated oven about 35 minutes, until dough is cooked through center and crust is lightly browned.

Transfer to a rack, brush again with reserved olive oil, and let cool about 15 minutes before cutting into thick slices.

Makes one large loaf.

THE ULTIMATE PIZZA BREAD, WITH SWEET ONION, PEPPERONI AND MOZZARELLA FILLING

A virtual Italian opera of flavors. An elegant alternative to a mundane sandwich, or a perfect accompaniment to a symphony of greens. We call it "Slice and Have Another" pizza bread, just perfect with a glass of Chianti.

Basic Pizza Bread dough
3 tablespoons olive oil
3 or 4 large, sweet Spanish
  onions, peeled and sliced,
  slices cut into thin slivers
½ small green pepper, seeded,
  chopped
2 cloves garlic, peeled, minced
4 or 5 thinly sliced pepperoni
  (about 2 oz.) cut into thin
  strips

4 oz. shredded mozzarella
  cheese
2 tablespoons grated Parmesan
  cheese
12 pimiento-stuffed green
  olives, sliced
Beaten egg

Prepare Basic Pizza Bread dough and set aside to rise.

Pour oil into a large, heavy skillet over low heat. Add onions and cook, stirring occasionally, about 25 minutes until very tender. Remove with slotted spoon and set aside. In same skillet stir-fry green pepper and garlic only until crisp-tender. Add pepperoni and toss in skillet for about 1 minute or until pepperoni is heated. Remove skillet from heat; pour off oil. Set aside.

When dough has risen, punch down and turn out on a lightly floured surface. Form into a ball; let stand about 20 minutes. Spread top of dough very lightly with flour, turn it over and with floured hands flatten it out into a 12" x 16" rectangle. Sprinkle with about half of the two cheeses. Spread vegetable and pepperoni mixture over dough, leaving 1½" border all around. Sprinkle with olives and remaining cheese. Turn up short ends to overlap filling. Beginning with long side, roll up jelly roll fashion. Pinch dough to seal. Place seam side up on a long, flat baking sheet. With a small, sharp knife slash top in several places to allow steam to escape. Let stand at room temperature about 30 minutes.

Preheat oven to 400° F.

Brush top of loaf with beaten egg. Bake in preheated oven 30 to 35 minutes or until crust is lightly browned. Transfer to a rack and let cool about 15 minutes before cutting into thick slices.

Makes one large loaf.

PIZZE FRITTE

We are told that pizze fritte *(fried pizza dough) was first developed by Italian bakers from dough left over after their bread loaves were first shaped and set aside for a second rising.* Pizze fritte *look like miniature golden harvest moons, and they taste as good as they look. Serve them hot from the pan, topped with a scarlet red sauce and sprinkled with cheese; or make the dough late in the day, let it rise, punch it down and place it in the refrigerator until the next morning, when you can let it rise again to fry up and serve hot as a late breakfast treat.*

Basic Pizza Bread dough   Desired sauces and cheeses or
Oil for frying   sweet toppings

Prepare Basic Pizza Bread dough and let rise until volume doubles.

When dough has risen, punch down and turn out on a lightly floured work surface. Knead 2 or 3 minutes, adding additional flour if needed to keep dough from sticking. Divide

23

dough into eight equal parts. Form each into a ball. With floured hands form each ball into a flat, round disk, about 5" to 6" in diameter.

Pour a thin layer of oil into a small skillet or crêpe pan just large enough to hold one pizza. Place over high heat. When oil is very hot, add a pizza. Fry, turning once, until lightly browned on both sides. Transfer to paper towel to drain. Set aside while preparing remaining pizzas. Serve hot with desired toppings.

Makes 8 pizzas.

ZESTY TOMATO-MUSHROOM TOPPING FOR PIZZE FRITTE

3 or 4 large sun-ripened
  tomatoes
1 tablespoon olive oil
1 small onion, peeled, chopped
6 to 8 large mushrooms,
  trimmed, chopped
1 clove garlic, peeled, minced
1 tablespoon minced parsley
1 tablespoon minced fresh basil
  or ¼ teaspoon dried basil

¼ teaspoon dried oregano
Salt to taste
Coarsely ground black pepper
  to taste
2 or 3 flat anchovy filets,
  drained, blotted dry, cut
  across into small slivers
Grated Parmesan or shredded
  mozzarella cheese (optional)

Cut each tomato in half; gently squeeze each half to remove seeds and juice. Chop halves into narrow strips; blot dry.

Pour oil into a small skillet, and place over low heat. Add tomato strips, onion and mushrooms. Sauté only until vegetables are crisp-tender. Stir in garlic and cook, stirring, until fragrant. Stir in herbs. Season very lightly with salt (remembering that anchovies are salty). Add pepper to taste; stir in anchovies. Cook, stirring, until heated, or set aside and reheat just before using.

Spoon over pizzas and, if desired, sprinkle with choice of cheeses just before serving.

Makes sufficient topping for 8 pizzas.

CHERRY SAUCE FOR *PIZZE FRITTE*

You might want to keep a jar of this sauce in the refrigerator for whenever you are in the mood to make pizze fritte.

1 1-lb. can dark, pitted cherries	⅓ cup honey
¼ cup juice from cherries	2 tablespoons butter
2 tablespoons cornstarch	½ teaspoon lemon extract
1 tablespoon grated orange rind	Remaining juice from cherries

Drain cherries through a colander set over a bowl. Set cherries aside. Pour ¼ cup cherry juice into a saucepan and stir in cornstarch. When smooth, add orange rind, honey, butter and lemon extract. Cook over low heat until smooth. Pour in remaining cherry juice. Increase heat and stir until mixture comes to a boil; cook and stir about 2 minutes. Stir in cherries. Serve hot or cold.

Makes sufficient sauce for 8 pizzas.

BREAKFAST TOPPING FOR *PIZZE FRITTE*

1 cup ricotta cheese	1 teaspoon grated lemon or
1 cup thick applesauce	orange zest

Combine ingredients; blend well. Chill in refrigerator until time to spoon over hot-from-the-skillet pizzas.

Makes sufficient topping for 8 pizzas.

● NEW GENERATION ITALIAN-AMERICAN PIZZA BREAD

This pizza bread dough is made in a slightly different way and is filled with crisp-cooked bacon and finely chopped

*green onions. Cut and used to make sandwiches with thick
slices of sun-ripened tomatoes, it's an Italian-American BLT.*

6 oz. thick-sliced bacon, cut across into thin strips	1 package dry yeast
1 small bunch green onions, including green parts, trimmed, chopped	¼ teaspoon sugar
	½ teaspoon salt
	1 cup all-purpose flour
1 cup warm water (105° to 110° F)	1½ cups additional flour
	Additional flour, as needed

In a large, heavy skillet cook bacon over low heat until crisp
and all fat rendered; with slotted spoon transfer to paper towels; set aside to drain. Add onions to rendered fat in skillet,
sauté until just tender. Remove with slotted spoon to paper
towels to drain. Set aside. Reserve rendered bacon fat.

In a large mixing bowl, combine water, yeast, sugar and
salt. Let stand until yeast has dissolved and mixture is bubbly.
Stir in one cup of flour and blend well. Stir in cooked bacon,
green onions and 1 tablespoon of the reserved rendered bacon
fat. (Refrigerate remaining rendered fat for other use.) Beat
with electric mixer at high speed or stir vigorously for 1 minute. Add remaining flour and stir to a soft dough. Turn out
on a lightly floured work surface and knead, adding additional
flour as necessary, until smooth and elastic. Form into a ball,
place in a lightly greased bowl, turn to coat all sides. Cover
bowl with plastic wrap or a clean dish towel, and set aside in
a warm, draft-free place until volume doubles.

Preheat oven to 400° F.

Punch dough down and turn it out on an inverted 12"
pizza pan or a baking sheet. With the heel of your hand spread
dough out evenly into a circle about 11" in diameter. Cover
lightly with a clean dish towel and let stand for about 20 minutes. Bake in preheated oven 25 to 30 minutes or until deep
golden. Serve warm or at room temperature.

Makes one 11" round loaf.

• PIZZA BREAD WITH SAUSAGE FILLING

Here's another hearty bread to round out a soup or salad meal. This one cuts corners by using commercially prepared frozen bread dough.

1 1-lb. loaf commercial frozen bread dough
Olive oil
1 lb. mild bulk sausage meat
1 small onion, peeled, minced
1 small clove garlic, peeled, minced
½ teaspoon oregano
½ teaspoon basil
½ teaspoon coarsely ground black pepper
½ teaspoon salt
1 1-lb. can Italian-style tomatoes
6 oz. shredded mozzarella cheese
2 tablespoons freshly grated Parmesan cheese
1 egg, beaten

Spread frozen bread dough lavishly with olive oil. Place in a large bowl. Cover bowl with plastic wrap and place in a warm, draft-free place for about 4 hours, until dough has thawed and is double in bulk.

While dough rises, prepare filling. In a large, heavy skillet fry sausage over medium heat, breaking it up as it cooks, about 15 minutes, until browned. Add onion and garlic; cook, stirring, until tender. Tilt skillet and spoon off all possible rendered fat. Stir in oregano, basil, pepper and salt.

Drain tomatoes through a colander set over a small bowl (reserve liquid for other use); add to sausage mixture and break up with the tip of a spatula or wooden spoon. Stir to blend ingredients. Set aside.

When dough has risen, turn out on a lightly floured surface; spread top of dough lightly but evenly with flour. Press out into a 15″ x 12″ rectangle. Place on long, flat baking sheet. Leaving a 1½″ border on the two short sides, spread the sausage mixture in a 4″ band down the center of dough. Cover with cheeses.

Fold the two short ends of the dough up and over the

filling. Moisten the long edges of dough with some of the beaten egg and pull up to completely enclose the filling, overlapping by about 1″ on top; press gently to seal. Let stand about 30 minutes.

Preheat oven to 400° F.

Brush top of dough with some of the beaten egg and with a small, sharp knife slash in several places to allow the steam to escape.

Bake in preheated oven about 35 minutes, until cooked through center and crust is lightly browned.

Transfer to a rack and let cool about 15 minutes before cutting into thick slices.

Makes one large loaf.

● SALT-FREE PIZZA BREAD

Mellowed garlic and fragrant herbs season this golden loaf. Salt? Who needs it?

3 tablespoons olive oil
1 large clove garlic, peeled, crushed
¾ cup warm water (105° to 110° F)
2 teaspoons sugar
1 package dry yeast
3 cups unbleached all-purpose white flour or 2½ cups semolina (durum wheat flour)

1 tablespoon finely chopped fresh basil or ½ teaspoon dried basil
½ teaspoon finely chopped fresh rosemary or ¼ teaspoon dried rosemary
Additional water, as needed
Additional flour, as needed

Pour oil into a small skillet over low heat; add garlic and cook, stirring occasionally, until deep golden and fragrant. Remove skillet from heat and discard garlic. Set aside. In a large mixing bowl, combine water, sugar and yeast. Stir once, let stand until bubbly. Add 1 cup flour. Stir in the garlic-flavored oil.

Add basil and rosemary. Beat to a smooth batter. Stir in remaining flour to form a soft dough that will pull away from sides of bowl. If too dry, sprinkle with a little additional water.

Turn dough out on a lightly floured work surface and let stand while you wash, dry and lightly oil the bowl.

Sprinkle dough lightly with flour, punch down, then with floured hands knead until smooth and elastic, adding additional flour as needed to keep dough from sticking. Form into a ball and place in oiled bowl. Turn to coat dough evenly. Cover bowl with plastic wrap and place in warm, draft-free place for 1½ to 2 hours, until dough doubles in volume.

Preheat oven to 400° F. Punch dough down and turn it out onto an inverted pizza pan or baking sheet. With your hands, spread dough out evenly into a circle about 11" in diameter. Cover lightly with a clean dish towel and let stand in a warm, draft-free place for about 30 minutes.

Bake in preheated oven for 20 to 25 minutes or until crust is deep golden. Serve warm or at room temperature.

Makes one 11" round loaf.

● DEEP-FRIED PIZZA BREAD STICKS

We like to prepare sufficient dough for two pizzas, using one half for a supper-time pizza, the other for these "better than store bought" Italian-style bread sticks.

All-Purpose Pizza Dough for one 12" to 14" round pizza (see Chapter 3)	Oil for frying Salt

Prepare dough and let rise until volume doubles. Punch down and turn out onto a lightly floured work surface; knead for 2 or 3 minutes. Divide dough into 4 equal parts. With your hands roll and stretch each part into a rope about 12" long.

Pour oil into a deep, heavy skillet until it reaches a depth of about 2″. Place over medium heat and bring to 350° F on a deep-fat thermometer. (At this temperature a small ball of dough will brown in about 1 minute.) Working one at a time, cut each rope of dough across into finger-length pieces; twist lightly, then drop into hot oil. Fry twisted strips a few at a time until pale, golden brown. Transfer to paper towels. Sprinkle lightly with salt. Repeat until all dough has been used.

Serve warm or at room temperature.

Makes about 4 dozen bread sticks.

Note: Bread sticks will stay fresh at room temperature for several hours. They may be refrigerated in airtight plastic bags for several days, or frozen on flat surface in freezer until firm, then stored in airtight freezer storage bags until ready to re-heat and serve.

3

Pizza Dough:
How to Make It,
Shape It and
Bake It

Although pie and pastry crust can be tricky, sometimes down-right difficult to make, nothing could be easier than preparing a glorious base for an elegant pizza. Better yet, it's fun to do: mixing takes only a few minutes, and unlike other yeast dough, pizza dough requires only one brief rising.

It's nice to know, too, that no yeast dough is less temperamental. If you're not ready to use the dough once it has doubled in volume, you can punch it down and let it rise a second time before proceeding. Or, if you prefer, you can make the dough, let it rise, punch it down and place it in the refrigerator for as long as two days, then bring it out and let it rise once more before making your pizza.

Another way to make pizza easier than pie is to knead and shape the dough as soon as it has risen and bake it for about 10 minutes in an oven preheated to 400° F. Allow dough to cool, place in freezer until firm, then wrap for freezer storage. No need to defrost before covering with desired sauce and toppings. Bake for 20 to 25 minutes in a preheated 375° F oven until the crust is brown and crisp, the sauce bubbly and the cheese melted. Or, as I'm sure you realize if you've ever purchased a commercially-prepared frozen pizza, you can make and bake a filled pizza, cool it, and freeze it; then, without defrosting, it can be reheated.

No matter how you plan to shape and bake these doughs, we guarantee you'll be pleased with the results.

ALL-PURPOSE PIZZA DOUGHS
Any of the doughs in this section can be used when a recipe calls for "all-purpose pizza dough."

● TRADITIONAL DOUGHS

Here are four variations—two using unbleached flour, one using semolina and one using a combination of Ceresota flour and semolina pasta flour.

ALL-PURPOSE PIZZA DOUGHS MADE WITH UNBLEACHED FLOUR
It takes only minutes to make these great-tasting, crispy-crust pizza doughs.

¼ cup warm water (105° to 110° F)

½ teaspoon sugar

½ teaspoon salt

½ package dry yeast

¼ cup additional warm water (105° to 110° F)

1 teaspoon olive oil, room temperature

1½ cups unbleached all-purpose flour

Additional water, as needed

Additional flour, as needed

Makes sufficient dough for one 12" to 14" round pizza, two 7" to 8" round pizzas, one oblong pizza or one dozen appetizer-size pizzas.

¼ cup warm water (105° to 110° F)

1 teaspoon sugar

1 teaspoon salt

1 package dry yeast

¾ cup additional warm water (105° to 110° F)

1 tablespoon olive oil, room temperature

3 cups unbleached all-purpose flour

Additional water, as needed

Additional flour, as needed

Makes sufficient dough for two 12" to 14" round pizzas, four 5" to 6" round pizzas, two oblong pizzas or two dozen appetizer-size pizzas.

ALL-PURPOSE PIZZA DOUGH MADE WITH SEMOLINA

This dough makes a chewy, "fulsome," authentically Italian crust with a light golden rim and a flavor slightly reminiscent of San Francisco's sourdough bread.

¼ cup warm water (105° to 110° F)

1 teaspoon sugar

1 teaspoon salt

1 package dry yeast

¾ cup additional warm water (105° to 110° F)

1 tablespoon olive oil, room temperature

2½ cups semolina (durum wheat flour)

Additional water, as needed

Additional flour, as needed

Makes sufficient dough for two 12" to 14" round pizzas, four 7" to 8" round pizzas, two oblong pizzas or two dozen appetizer-size pizzas.

ALL-PURPOSE PIZZA DOUGH MADE WITH CERESOTA FLOUR AND SEMOLINA

Ceresota flour is an excellent blend of hard and soft wheats. The addition of coarsely ground semolina pasta flour gives the crust a sunny Italian flavor.

¼ cup warm water (105° to 110° F)

1 teaspoon sugar

1 teaspoon salt

1 package dry yeast

¾ cup additional warm water (105° to 110° F)

1 tablespoon olive oil, room temperature

2 cups Ceresota (or Heckers brand) unbleached all-purpose flour

½ cup coarsely ground semolina pasta flour

Additional water, as needed

Additional flour, as needed

Makes sufficient dough for two 12" to 14" round pizzas, four 7" to 8" round pizzas, two oblong pizzas or two dozen appetizer-size pizzas.

34

MIXING AND KNEADING

Pizza dough can be prepared by hand, with a food processor or with an electric mixer and dough hook.

Hand Method. Pour ¼ cup water into a medium-size bowl; stir in sugar and salt. Sprinkle yeast over surface, and stir once; let stand about 5 minutes, until mixture is bubbly. Stir in remaining warm water and the oil.

Place flour in a large mixing bowl; add yeast mixture. Stir to a soft dough that will pull away from sides of bowl. If too dry, sprinkle with a little more water.

Turn dough out on a well-floured work surface; sprinkle top with additional flour. Punch down with the heels of your hands, then fold over. Knead by pressing the dough down again, pushing it out a bit and folding it over from the other side, adding flour as needed to keep it from sticking. When it becomes springy, very smooth, light and elastic, form into a smooth ball.

Food Processor Method. Pour ¼ cup water in work bowl of food processor. Sprinkle with sugar, salt and yeast. Process 30 seconds; let stand about 5 minutes until bubbly. Add remaining water and the oil. Process 30 seconds. Add flour, cover and process about 7 seconds or until 1 or 2 balls of dough form on the blade. If balls will not form, mixture is too dry; add a few drops more water.

Turn dough out on a well floured work surface; sprinkle top lightly with additional flour. Knead about 3 minutes or until dough is smooth and elastic, adding flour as needed to keep dough from sticking. Form into a smooth ball.

Electric Mixer with Dough Hook Method. Pour ¼ cup water into a medium-size bowl; stir in sugar and salt. Sprinkle yeast over surface; let stand about 5 minutes until bubbly. Stir in remaining water and the oil. Place flour in a large mixing bowl. With mixer at low speed, gradually pour yeast mixture into flour. Knead according to manufacturer's directions 15 to 20 minutes, until dough has massed on hook and becomes smooth. If too dry to mass, add a few drops of water. If dough starts to climb onto head of mixer, sprinkle with 1 or 2 tablespoons flour. If dough does not cling to hook after about 5 minutes, beater height may need to be adjusted; check manufacturer's directions.

Turn dough out onto floured work surface; knead about 3 minutes. Form into a smooth ball.

● ALL-PURPOSE SALT-FREE PIZZA DOUGH

Just because you are on a low-sodium diet doesn't mean you must forego the pleasures of pizza. You can use this dough for the main-course salt-free pizza you'll find in Chapter 5; or, if you eliminate the salt from the stuffings, you can use it for many kinds of calzones.

1 tablespoon olive oil
1 clove garlic, peeled, crushed
¼ cup warm water (105° to 110° F)
1 teaspoon sugar
1 package dry yeast
¾ cup additional warm water (105° to 110° F)

3 cups unbleached all-purpose flour or 2½ cups semolina
¼ teaspoon dried basil
¼ teaspoon dried oregano
¼ teaspoon dried rosemary
Additional water, as needed
Additional flour, as needed

Pour oil into a small skillet; add garlic and place over very low heat. Cook, stirring occasionally, until garlic is tender and very lightly browned. Remove and discard garlic; bring oil to room temperature.

Pour ¼ cup water into a large mixing bowl; stir in sugar, and sprinkle with yeast. Let stand until yeast has dissolved and mixture is bubbly. Stir in remaining water and the room-temperature oil. Add 1 cup flour, the basil, oregano and rosemary. Beat to a smooth batter. Stir in remaining flour, and mix until dough will come away from sides of bowl and can be formed into a soft ball. If dough is too dry, sprinkle with a little additional water. If it is too moist, knead in a little more flour. Turn ball of dough out onto a floured work surface and knead until smooth and elastic, adding additional flour only if dough sticks to work surface. Form into a smooth ball.

Makes sufficient dough for two 10″ to 12″ round pizzas, 4 plate-size pizzas, 2 Palermo-style pizzas or 2 calzones.

● ALL-PURPOSE PIZZA DOUGH WITH STARTER

A sponge "starter" lends a lightness to this dough. Rye flour adds intriguing flavor and texture.

1 package dry yeast
½ teaspoon sugar
½ cup warm water (105° to 110° F)
½ cup unbleached all-purpose flour
¾ cup additional warm water (105° to 110° F)

3 tablespoons olive oil
1½ teaspoons salt
3½ cups additional unbleached all-purpose flour
3 tablespoons rye flour
Additional water, as needed
Additional all-purpose flour, as needed

In a large bowl, sprinkle yeast and sugar over warm water. Stir once, then let stand until yeast has dissolved and mixture is bubbly. Stir in ½ cup all-purpose flour. Cover bowl with plastic wrap or a clean dish towel. Set aside in a warm, draft-free place about 45 minutes, until mixture expands and is bubbling actively.

Uncover bowl and gently fold in remaining water, oil and salt. Stir in remaining all-purpose flour and rye flour. Mix to a smooth, soft dough that will come away from sides of bowl and form into a ball. If too dry, sprinkle with a little additional water. Turn dough out on a lightly floured work surface. Knead until smooth and elastic, adding additional flour as necessary to keep dough from sticking. Form into a ball.

Makes sufficient dough for two 10″ to 12″ round pizzas, four 7″ to 8″ round pizzas, one oblong pizza or two dozen appetizer-size pizzas.

ALL YOU NEED TO KNOW ABOUT RISING, SHAPING AND BAKING YOUR PIZZA DOUGH

● RISING

Lightly grease a large bowl with oil. Place ball of dough in bowl and turn to coat all sides. Cover bowl with plastic wrap or a clean dish towel. Let rise in a warm, draft-free place until double in volume. (This will take from 1½ to 2 hours, depending on ingredients used and temperature of kitchen.)

If dough rises before you are ready to use it, punch it down in the bowl, bring sides inward, turn it over and reshape into a ball. If top is dry, spread with a little additional oil. Let rise a second time before using. Or, if you prefer, you can punch the dough down, reshape it, cover the bowl and place it in the refrigerator for up to two days before letting it rise at room temperature.

For thin, crisp pizza crust: Punch dough down; turn out and shape in pizza pan, on baking sheet or on baker's peel. Cover with filling and topping and bake at once.

For thicker, softer pizza crust: Punch dough down; turn out and shape in pizza pan, on baking sheet or on baker's peel. Cover lightly with a clean dish towel and let rise about 30 minutes before covering with filling and topping.

● SHAPING AND BAKING

Pizza can be shaped and baked successfully either "home-style" (in a pizza pan) or "pizza shop fashion" (on a baking stone). The first method is quick and easy. The second is fun to do and, after a little practice, not nearly as difficult as it might seem at first.

HOME-STYLE PIZZA

Place rack on lowest position in oven. Preheat oven to 425° F. When dough has doubled in volume, punch it down and turn it out on a lightly floured work surface. Knead for a minute or so, working in a little flour if dough seems sticky. (If making more than one large pizza, divide dough into equal portions and work one at a time.) Flatten dough into a circle about 1" thick. Holding the circle up in your hands at one edge, stretch the dough by turning it and pulling your hands gently apart at the same time. When the circle is about 7" or 8" across, spread it out on the floured surface again and pat it smooth, pressing together any tears. Then lightly roll the dough with a rolling pin from the center to the far edge, turning it clockwise after each roll, until you have a circle of pastry about ½" larger in circumference than the pan you are going to use. Place the circle in the pan and press it out evenly to cover bottom and sides of pan.

For an oblong pizza: Roll the stretched-out dough into a rectangle just a little smaller than the long, shallow oblong pan you are going to use. Place dough in pan and press out evenly, covering bottom and sides of pan.

For small pizzas: Divide dough and shape into small balls. Flatten each ball with floured hands into a circle; place circles slightly apart on a long, flat baking sheet. Press edges of each circle up to form a slightly thick rim.

Whatever size pizzas you make and however you form them, add the filling and topping just before baking.

PIZZA SHOP PIZZA

Place a round or oblong baking stone on center rack of oven and preheat oven to 450° F.

Sprinkle a baker's peel or a sheet of heavy-duty cardboard lightly with cornmeal or semolina.

When the dough has doubled in volume, punch down and turn out on a lightly floured work surface. (If making more than one large pizza, divide dough into equal portions and work one at a time.) Knead for a minute or so, working in a little flour if it seems sticky. With the palm of your hand, flatten dough into a circle about 1" thick. Holding the circle up by one edge in your hands, turn and stretch the dough by holding the circle and pulling your hands gently apart at the same time. Again, spread it out on the floured surface and pat it smooth. Spread with a very thin film of flour, turn it over and spread with flour again. Flour backs of hands and, making two fists, cross them closely together under center of dough, forming flat surface for dough to rest on. Gradually pull fists apart, turning them simultaneously, to stretch dough. As center becomes thin, move fists further apart to stretch sides of dough. Repeat as necessary, being careful not to make dough too thin in center, until dough has reached the desired circumference.

Place on prepared baker's peel; reshape to an even circle. Crimp edges up to form a slight rim. Just before baking, place filling and topping on dough. Shake peel back and forth. If pizza does not move freely, slide long, flexible-blade spatula under dough to loosen it. To transfer pizza to preheated baking stone, pull out rack from preheated oven and, starting from back of baking stone, tip peel and ease far edge of pizza onto stone, then pull peel quickly out from under pizza, leaving it on stone. Reduce oven temperature to 425° F. Bake as directed. When pizza is baked, slip peel under crust and transfer to serving board.

Bake all pizzas from 15 to 20 minutes, until crust is lightly browned around edges, cheeses are melted and toppings are bubbly hot. Exact time depends on size and shape of pizza and type of topping (see individual recipes). For a crisper, browner crust, bake crust alone for 3 minutes before adding toppings.

TOSSING DOUGH TO SHAPE IT PROFESSIONAL PIZZA-MAKER FASHION

To toss or not to toss? Well, now, that depends on you and your style. If you like to cook for your family and friends while they watch and wait, or if they like to share in the fun, you may want to learn this art of the professional pizza baker. Even if you can't detect any difference in the final results, it will give you a sense of "pizza-making power." After having tossed a few, you may feel that when the phone rings you'll receive an order for "one with anchovies and one with extra cheese."

40

To toss pizza dough follow the directions above for pizza shop pizza. When dough has been pulled and shaped into a flat circle, flour the backs of your hands lightly and make two fists. Cross them close together under the center of the dough. Now here we go! Lift fists and toss dough upward while at the same time uncrossing wrist in a twisting motion to give dough a spin. Catch it on your fists and, pulling fists farther apart so sides of dough will be stretched when tossed, repeat two or three times more, pulling fists outward each time so that dough will not be too thin in center. Thin out edges by pulling dough between your fingers. It should be about ¼″ thick.

4

Special Sauces and Toppings for Pizza

In great cuisines throughout the world, sauce making and special extras, such as flavorful toppings, figure largely. Sauces and toppings are of special importance in Italian cookery, however. Although the recipes are usually simple, the results are simply superb.

If any one thing can elevate a pizza from ordinary to magnificent, it is one of these Italian-style sauces or special embellishments. The recipes here offer quite a variety of possibilities, and each can be seasoned to suit your own taste, made mild, lively, or extra hearty in flavor. Midsummer is the time to make a delicately delicious fresh-tomato sauce; but you can make a great sauce for pizza anytime, whether it is a double-thick meat topping, a piquant anchovy covering for a crisp pizza crust or a classic tomato sauce.

Although this chapter is short, it can go a long way toward making your pizza cookery easy and doubly delicious. Each recipe is both foolproof and economical. And none takes more than a short time to prepare; in fact, you can start any one of them after you have prepared your pizza dough and finish long before the dough has risen.

If you like, quantities can be doubled or tripled. Then, whatever you don't use immediately can be poured into 1- or 2-cup airtight containers and stored in your freezer—ready whenever you are. Use your leftover sauce or topping for yet another great pizza creation, to top a double-quick version, or to create a pizza-spin-off entrée.

● CLASSIC PIZZA SAUCE

A traditional, extremely flavorful sauce. This recipe makes enough for 2 or 3 pizzas and can be prepared ahead and stored in your refrigerator or freezer, ready when you are for quick-to-make pizzas.

3 tablespoons olive oil

1 small onion, peeled, finely chopped

2 cloves garlic, peeled, minced

1 28-oz. can Italian plum tomatoes and their juice

1 6-oz. can tomato paste

1 cup water

1 tablespoon minced fresh basil or 1 teaspoon dried basil

1 tablespoon minced fresh thyme or ½ to 1 teaspoon dried thyme

1 tablespoon minced fresh oregano or ½ to 1 teaspoon dried oregano

1 teaspoon sugar

1 teaspoon salt

1 tablespoon red wine vinegar

Pour oil into a large, heavy skillet over medium heat. When hot, add onions and sauté until transparent. Stir in garlic; continue to cook, stirring until garlic is soft but not brown. Add tomatoes and their juice. Cook, breaking up tomatoes with the tip of a wooden spoon or a spatula, until liquid begins to simmer. Stir in tomato paste and water. Add basil, thyme, oregano, sugar and salt. Bring to boil, then reduce heat and simmer, stirring occassionally, 35 to 45 minutes, until sauce is very thick. Stir in vinegar. Taste and adjust seasonings.

Makes about 4 cups of sauce.

Note: Bring sauce to room temperature before using. If desired, store in airtight 1- or 2-cup containers up to 1 week in refrigerator, 4 to 6 weeks in freezer.

● PIZZA SAUCE WITH FRESH TOMATOES

One of nature's greatest gifts in the summertime is an abundance of juicy, red, sun-ripened tomatoes. This is the time to put them to full use in a magnificent sauce for an extraordinarily flavorful pizza.

4 or 5 large, ripe tomatoes, about 2 lb.

2 tablespoons olive oil

1 large onion, peeled, finely chopped

1 6-oz. can tomato paste

2 tablespoons chopped fresh basil or 1 teaspoon dried basil

½ teaspoon dried oregano

1 tablespoon grated Parmesan cheese

Salt to taste

Freshly ground black pepper to taste

Bring a large pot of water to full boil. Add one tomato; let boil for about 10 seconds. Remove with long-handled fork, hold under running water, and peel off skin. Cut and discard core. Hold tomato over a large bowl and cut into chunks, letting juice fall into bowl. Repeat process with remaining tomatoes.

Pour oil into a large, heavy skillet over low heat. When hot, add onions and sauté about 5 minutes until transparent. Add tomato chunks and their juice. Cover; let chunks steam until mixture is very juicy. Stir in tomato paste. Add basil and oregano; cook, stirring occasionally, until mixture thickens. Stir in grated Parmesan. Season to taste with salt and pepper. Set aside at room temperature until ready to use, or refrigerate and then bring to room temperature before using.

Makes about 3 cups of sauce.

● TOMATO AND CREAM SAUCE

This creamy, smooth, rich sauce tastes positively superb when topped with a profusion of cheese and slivered black olives.

3 tablespoons butter
1 small onion, peeled, very finely minced
3 tablespoons very finely minced parsley
2 tablespoons flour

1 28-oz. can Italian-style tomatoes and their juice
1 teaspoon salt (more if desired)
1/4 teaspoon sugar
1/2 cup heavy cream

Melt butter in a large, heavy skillet over low heat. Add onion and parsley; cook, stirring, until onion is tender. Stir in flour until blended. Add tomatoes and their juice. Season with salt and sugar. Bring to boil; lower heat and let simmer until liquid is reduced by about half. Stir in cream; cook, stirring, until sauce is very thick and smooth.

Makes about 2 cups of sauce.

● GARLIC LOVERS' PIZZA SAUCE

3 tablespoons olive oil
1 medium onion, peeled, minced
1/2 small green pepper, seeded, minced
3 large cloves fresh garlic, peeled, finely minced
1 1/2 cups water
1 6-oz. can tomato paste

1 tablespoon chopped fresh basil or 1/2 teaspoon dried basil
1/2 teaspoon dried oregano
1 tablespoon minced parsley
Salt to taste
Pepper to taste
2 or 3 dashes hot pepper sauce (optional)

Pour oil into deep, heavy skillet over medium-high heat. Add onion and green pepper; cook and stir for about 5 minutes. Add garlic and continue to cook, stirring, until vegetables are tender. Add water; stir in tomato paste. Sprinkle sauce with basil, oregano and parsley. Lower heat and let simmer about 5 minutes. Add salt and pepper to taste. If desired, add hot pepper sauce. Let simmer, stirring often, about 30 minutes, until sauce is thick.

Makes about 3 cups, sufficient sauce for two 12″ to 14″ round pizzas, one oblong pizza or one deep-dish pizza.

●QUICK AND EASY TOMATO SAUCE FOR PIZZA

This is a basic sauce that can be seasoned with Italian herbs to suit your taste.

1 large onion, peeled, finely chopped

1 clove garlic, peeled, finely minced

2 tablespoons olive oil

1 28-oz. can Italian-style tomatoes and their juice

1 6-oz. can tomato paste

2 tomato paste cans of water

1 tablespoon red wine vinegar

¼ teaspoon sugar

1 teaspoon salt

¼ teaspoon coarsely ground black pepper

Choice of herbs: basil, oregano, marjoram, rosemary, etc.

In a large, heavy saucepan, sauté onions and garlic in oil until tender. Add tomatoes and their juice. Stir in tomato paste, water, vinegar and sugar. Season with salt, pepper and desired herbs. Cook over low heat, stirring occasionally, until sauce thickens.

Makes about 4 cups of sauce.

● QUICK PIZZA SAUCE

This sauce has a lovely homemade taste; but it's quick to prepare, can be seasoned to your taste, and can be made ahead and frozen to reappear weeks later. Now what more could you ask?

1 large onion, peeled, chopped
1 small green pepper, seeded, chopped
1 small carrot, scraped, minced
¼ lb. fresh mushrooms, trimmed, chopped
2 tablespoons vegetable or olive oil
2 1-lb. cans tomato sauce
½ cup water

Choice of herbs: minced fresh basil or dried basil, oregano, marjoram, rosemary, thyme
Salt to taste
Freshly ground black pepper to taste
1 tablespoon red wine vinegar, or slivers of lemon rind, or 1 to 2 tablespoons dry red wine (optional)

In a large Dutch oven or heavy pot, sauté onion, green pepper, carrot and mushrooms in oil over very low heat, about 5 minutes, until vegetables are tender. Add sauce and water. Add herbs of your choice and season with salt and pepper. Add vinegar, lemon rind or wine. Cook, stirring occasionally, about 10 to 15 minutes, until sauce is heated.

If desired, spoon into 1-cup airtight containers and store in refrigerator or freezer until ready to use.

Makes about 4 cups of sauce.

● INSTANT PIZZA SAUCE

This no-cook sauce is for those times when you're really in a panic for pizza.

1 6-oz. can tomato paste
1 tomato paste can of water
1 teaspoon mixed Italian
   seasonings

½ teaspoon dried oregano
1 teaspoon red wine vinegar

Combine ingredients; blend well.

    Makes 1½ cups, sufficient sauce for one 12″ to 14″ round pizza.

● PIQUANT ANCHOVY SAUCE

We like to cover prepared pizza dough with this sauce, bake for about 10 minutes, then cover it exuberantly with half skim-milk, half whole-milk mozzarella. You'll need nothing more to make an extremely flavorful pizza.

1 tablespoon olive oil
1 clove garlic, peeled, finely
   minced
1 2-oz. can anchovy filets,
   drained, chopped

1 28-oz. can Italian-style tomatoes and their juice
1 teaspoon tomato paste
Coarsely ground black pepper

In a large, heavy skillet over low heat, combine olive oil and garlic; cook, stirring, until fragrant. Add the chopped anchovy filets and cook, stirring, for about 30 seconds. Pour in tomatoes and their juice. Cook, breaking up tomatoes with the tip of a spoon, until liquid comes to a boil. Stir in tomato paste; cook, stirring frequently, until sauce thickens. Season to taste with pepper. No salt is needed, as the anchovies are extremely salty.

    Makes about 3 cups of sauce.

•ITALIAN MEAT SAUCE FOR PIZZA

1 lb. ground beef
1 large onion, peeled, finely chopped
1 medium green pepper, seeded, finely chopped
1 clove garlic, peeled, minced
1 28-oz. can Italian-style plum tomatoes and their juice
1 6-oz. can tomato paste
1 cup water

1 teaspoon dried oregano
2 tablespoons chopped fresh basil or 2 teaspoons dried basil
2 tablespoons grated Parmesan or Romano cheese
Salt to taste
Coarsely ground black pepper to taste

In a large, heavy skillet over medium heat, brown beef in its own fat, stirring to break up. Stir in onion and green pepper. Cook, stirring, about 5 minutes. Add garlic and continue to cook and stir another minute. Tilt pan; spoon off and discard excess rendered fat. Add tomatoes and their juice. With the tip of a wooden spoon or a spatula break tomatoes into chunks. Stir in tomato paste and water. Add oregano and basil. Lower heat; let simmer, stirring occasionally, until liquid thickens. Stir in grated cheese. Season to taste with salt and pepper. Set aside at room temperature until ready to use, or refrigerate until needed but bring to room temperature before using.

Makes about 4 cups of sauce.

● SAUCE BOLOGNESE

This sauce is so rich, thick and flavorful that your pizza needs only a slight sprinkling of Parmesan and mozzarella cheeses to complete its perfection.

2 tablespoons olive oil
2 tablespoons butter
1 large yellow onion, peeled, finely chopped
2 stalks celery, finely chopped
1 small carrot, scraped, finely chopped
1 lb. lean ground beef
¼ teaspoon salt
½ cup dry white wine
½ cup light cream or half-and-half

2 cups homemade fat-free beef stock, or 1 10½-oz. can beef broth and sufficient water to make 2 cups
1 28-oz. can Italian-style tomatoes and their juice
2 tablespoons flour
2 tablespoons butter
Additional salt
Coarsely ground black pepper

Pour oil into a large, heavy saucepan; add butter. Place over low heat until butter has melted. Add onion, celery and carrot. Cook, stirring occasionally, for about 10 minutes.

Add ground beef and salt. Cook, stirring, until meat is no longer pink. Pour in wine, turn heat to medium high and cook, stirring occasionally, until all the wine has evaporated. Reduce heat, add cream and cook, stirring, until mixture is almost dry. Add tomatoes and cook, breaking them up with the tip of a spoon, until liquid comes to a full boil. Add beef stock or broth. Reduce heat even further and let mixture simmer very gently for about 1 hour.

In a small bowl, combine flour and butter. Mash with a fork until blended and mixture can be formed into a small ball. Add this to the sauce; stir until it has dissolved and sauce is very thick. Season with salt and pepper to taste.

Makes about 4 cups of sauce.

Note: This sauce can be kept in the refrigerator for 2 or 3 days, or it can be put into 1-cup freezer containers and kept frozen until ready to use. Thaw in top half of double boiler over simmering water. Cool to room temperature before using for pizza.

● MEXICAN SALSA

Serve this piquant fresh-tomato sauce over Mexican pizzas.

1 large, juicy, ripe tomato
1 small onion, peeled, finely
  chopped (about ¼ cup)
1 tablespoon finely chopped
  parsley (Italian parsley preferred)

3 Serrano or other hot chilis,
  seeded and finely chopped, or
  ¼ cup canned green chilis,
  finely chopped
½ teaspoon salt
Coarsely ground black pepper

Holding tomato over bowl, cut into chunks, letting chunks and juice drop into bowl. Use a small knife to chop chunks into fine pieces. Stir in remaining ingredients, adding pepper to taste. Cover; let stand about 30 minutes at room temperature before serving. Make this sauce no more than 2 to 3 hours before serving, as it soon loses its crispness and flavor.

Makes about ¾ cup salsa.

● PESTO FOR PIZZA

Stir pesto into a mild tomato sauce for a pizza topping you will long remember. Or spread it on pizza dough, cover dough with fresh tomatoes and top with slices of cheese; bake and enjoy. You can also spoon pesto over the last topping just before your pizza is baked, or serve it separately to spoon over baked pizza.

3 cups fresh basil leaves,
  washed, drained and tightly
  packed
¼ cup chopped parsley (Italian
  parsley preferred)
½ cup olive oil

1 tablespoon finely minced
  garlic
½ cup pignoli nuts
1 teaspoon salt
½ cup Parmesan cheese

52

Place all ingredients in container of food processor or electric blender; process or blend until smooth. Use the pesto at once; or spoon it into a storage container and cover with about ½ inch olive oil, cover tightly and store in refrigerator until ready to use.

Makes about 2 cups of pesto.

● PARSLEY PESTO

This flavorful variation of pesto can be made year round from readily available parsley and dried basil.

1 small bunch parsley (about 1 cup parsley leaves)	2 teaspoons dried basil
	¼ cup Parmesan cheese
2 cloves garlic, peeled, coarsely chopped	¼ cup olive or vegetable oil

Rinse parsley clean under cold running water; blot dry. Remove and discard tough stems.

Place parsley and remaining ingredients in work bowl of food processor or blender. Process or blend until smooth.

Makes about 1 cup of pesto.

●MIDSUMMER PIZZA TOPPING

This recipe came about on a lazy, hot, summer day when there was an abundance of sun-ripened tomatoes and fresh basil in our garden. Delicious!

6 large sun-ripened tomatoes
1 lb. shredded mozzarella
   cheese
½ cup chopped fresh basil
   leaves
4 to 6 large mushrooms,
   coarsely chopped (optional)

¼ cup olive oil
1 teaspoon salt (or to taste)
A generous sprinkling of
   coarsely ground black pepper

Wash and core tomatoes, but do not remove skins. One at a time, hold over a bowl and cut into large chunks, letting chunks and juice fall into bowl. Stir in remaining ingredients. Let stand at room temperature about 2 hours before using.

Makes sufficient topping for one 12″ to 14″ round pizza.

●MEATBALLS WITH PARMESAN CHEESE

These flavorful miniature meatballs can be prepared ahead, ready to glorify your pizza at a moment's notice.

3 thick slices Italian bread
¼ cup tomato juice, chicken
   broth or water
½ lb. ground beef
½ lb. ground pork
½ lb. ground veal
2 tablespoons grated Parmesan
   cheese

2 eggs
1 teaspoon salt
½ teaspoon coarsely ground
   black pepper
¼ teaspoon Italian seasoning
Oil for frying

54

Preheat oven to 250° F.

Place the bread slices on center rack in oven until dry. Crumble slices and place in work bowl of food processor or blender. Process or blend to fine crumbs. Transfer to a small bowl. Pour in tomato juice or other liquid. Let stand about 5 minutes.

In a large bowl combine beef, pork and veal. Stir in cheese, eggs, salt, pepper and Italian seasoning. Squeeze bread crumbs dry and add to meat mixture. Blend thoroughly. With moistened fingers, shape into 18 to 20 small balls.

Pour oil into a deep, heavy skillet until it reaches a depth of about ½". Place over medium heat. When oil is hot, add meatballs a few at a time and cook, turning frequently, until brown on all sides.

Meatballs can be prepared ahead. Drain on paper towels, and store in refrigerator until ready to use (no more than 24 hours). Or place in a single layer on a long, flat baking sheet in freezer until firm. Transfer to an airtight freezer container, and store in freezer up to 1 month. Reheat in pizza or tomato sauce.

Makes 18 to 20 meatballs.

● ITALIAN MEATBALLS WITH MORTADELLA

The flavor of these meatballs is heightened by the addition of imported Italian mortadella. They make a great topping for just about any pizza.

1 lb. ground beef
½ lb. finely minced mortadella
¾ cup dried bread crumbs
¼ cup tomato juice
1 egg

1 small onion, peeled, finely minced
1½ teaspoons salt
¼ teaspoon ground pepper
⅛ teaspoon dried basil

Mix beef with mortadella, bread crumbs, tomato juice, egg, onion, salt, pepper and basil. Blend well. Shape mixture into ½" balls (dipping hands in cold water from time to time for easy shaping).

Preheat oven to 350° F.

Arrange meatballs on a long, shallow baking sheet so that they are not touching each other. Bake in preheated oven for 10 minutes. Turn each ball and bake another 10 minutes or until lightly browned.

Makes about 48 meatballs.

Note: Meatballs can be made ahead. Arrange on a flat surface, not touching each other. Place in freezer until firm. Store in airtight container until ready to use.

Reheat in pizza or tomato sauce.

● SAUSAGE TOPPING FOR PIZZA

The advantage of making your own sausage topping is that you can adjust the seasoning to your taste.

1 lb. mild bulk ground sausage

1 cup homemade tomato sauce or 1 8-oz. can mild tomato sauce

Choice of herbs: fresh or dried basil, oregano, rosemary, marjoram

Salt to taste

Coarsely ground black pepper to taste

In a large, heavy skillet over medium heat cook sausage, stirring frequently, until lightly browned. Spoon off rendered fat. Add tomato sauce, choice of herbs, salt and pepper. Cook, stirring frequently, until all liquid has been absorbed but mixture is still slightly moist.

Makes sufficient topping for one 12" to 14" round pizza.

5

Great Big
Beautiful Pizzas

Cooking can be terribly dull, and meals can become a bore. But serve a classic Pizza Margherita, an American-style pizza with a variety of toppings, a calzone or a double-crusted, double-delicious Palermo-style *sfinciuni*, and kitchen chores become fun, dull meals a thing of the past.

During the last few years we have been asked time after time for the "how to" of great big beautiful pizza making. So we have taken all the most requested recipes, retested them for accuracy, made them quick and easy to prepare, and put them together in this chapter. Choose one, add an easy-to-make antipasto platter or a beautiful salad of mixed greens, plus a light fruit dessert, and your meal is prepared.

We've included some well-known classic pizzas here, and many others you probably have not heard of. But we can guarantee—having made and served each one many times—that you, your family and your guests will like them all. Each one captures the flavor and hearty aroma of truly great Italian cookery. Pizzas are, for a fact, among the world's best liked almost-one-dish meals. If you don't believe it now, you will after trying just one of these recipes. You will discover, as we did, that when you start with a pizza, menu planning can actually be fun.

And it's so easy! Pizza dough is extremely simple to make. We guarantee it will give you no disastrous surprises. A pizza sauce can be put together in a matter of minutes. The toppings for pizza are as simple as old-fashioned arithmetic: add or subtract as you like. And once you have put your pizza together, the baking is surprisingly quick. The only thing left is the pleasure of serving one of the best meals you can possibly prepare.

Just buy a pizza chef's hat and begin. You'll love it.

● PIZZA MARGHERITA

(Pizza Neapolitan Style)

This classic Neapolitan creation was named in honor of Princess Margherita of Italy. It is undoubtedly the best-known and most popular of all pizzas.

All-Purpose Pizza Dough for two 12″ to 14″ round pizzas (see Chapter 3)

4 lb. vine-ripened tomatoes or 4 1-lb. cans Italian-style plum tomatoes, drained

4 tablespoons grated Parmesan or Romano cheese

1½ lb. shredded mozzarella cheese

6 to 8 tablespoons additional grated Parmesan or Romano cheese

Embellishments:

Pepperoni slices

Domestic or Genoa salami, sliced

Cooked Italian sausage, thinly sliced or crumbled

Anchovy filets or rolled caper-stuffed anchovy filets

Prosciutto or soppressata

Sliced fresh mushrooms, raw or lightly sautéed

Bite-size meatballs

Green peppers, cut into strips or rings

Oil-cured, Italian-style ripe olives, pitted and halved or cut into slivers

Fontina cheese strips

Provolone cheese, cut into slivers

Additional mozzarella cheese

Additional Parmesan or Romano cheese

Prepare pizza dough. While dough rises, prepare toppings.

If using fresh tomatoes, plunge them, a few at a time, into a large pot of rapidly boiling water. Hold under cold running water and slip off skins. Cut each in half and squeeze out all juice and seeds. Cut halves into large chunks; blot thoroughly dry. Set aside. If using canned tomatoes, drain them in a colander set over a bowl. Reserve juice for other use. Blot tomatoes thoroughly dry and chop them into large pieces.

Bring all other ingredients to room temperature.

If preparing pizzas on a baking stone, place stone on center rack in oven and preheat oven to 450° F. If preparing pizzas in pizza pans, place rack on lowest position in oven. Preheat oven to 425° F. When dough has risen, punch it down and turn it out on a lightly floured work surface.

If preparing two home-style pizzas, divide dough in half. Knead, flatten and shape one half in pizza pan. Sprinkle with 2 tablespoons of grated Parmesan or Romano cheese. Cover with half of the fresh or canned tomatoes. Bake in preheated oven for about 5 minutes. Top with any one, two or three embellishments; cover with half the shredded mozzarella cheese and about 2 more tablespoons of grated Parmesan or Romano cheese. Bake about 20 minutes, until cheeses are melted and crust is lightly browned. Remove from oven and let stand while you prepare second pizza. (First pizza will remain hot while second is prepared.)

Makes two 12" to 14" round pizzas.

If preparing pizzas on baker's peel for baking on a preheated stone, divide dough into 4 equal portions. One at a time, knead, flatten and shape each portion on baker's peel. Sprinkle dough evenly with Parmesan cheese, and top with fresh or canned tomatoes. Slide pizza from peel onto heated baking stone. Reduce oven temperature to 425° F. Bake about 5 minutes. Top with any one, two or three embellishments; sprinkle evenly with shredded mozzarella and top with grated Parmesan or Romano cheese. Bake about 15 or 20 minutes, until cheeses are melted and crust is lightly browned. Slide baker's peel under pizza on stone and transfer to serving board. Repeat with remaining dough, cheeses, tomatoes and embellishments until all pizzas are baked. Serve each pizza as baked or reheat briefly in a 350° F oven just before serving.

Makes 4 plate-size pizzas.

● PIZZA ALLA MARINARA

(Pizza with garlic, tomatoes and olive oil)

This traditional Neapolitan pizza contains no cheese. For best flavor, use large, fresh cloves of sweet garlic from California and fresh, sun-ripened tomatoes.

All-Purpose Pizza Dough for one
    12″ to 14″ round pizza (see
    Chapter 3)
3 or 4 very large sun-ripened
    tomatoes (about 1½ lb.)
Salt
4 tablespoons olive oil

3 large cloves garlic, peeled,
    very thinly sliced
1 teaspoon oregano
4 to 6 large fresh mushrooms,
    trimmed, thinly sliced
6 to 8 pitted Kalamata olives,
    cut into slivers

Prepare pizza dough. Set aside to rise.

Trim ends from tomatoes; cut into thick slices. Place slices in single layer on a double thickness of paper towels. Sprinkle evenly with salt; let stand about 10 minutes, turn, sprinkle again with salt and let stand until ready to use.

Pour oil into a small, heavy skillet; add garlic and oregano. Cook over very low heat until garlic is tender and mixture fragrant. Set aside.

If baking pizza on preheated baking stone, place stone on center rack in oven and preheat oven to 450° F. If baking pizza in pizza pan, place rack on lowest position in oven and preheat oven to 425° F.

When dough has risen, punch down and turn out on a lightly floured surface. Flatten out and shape, as directed, in pizza pan or on baker's peel. (If shaping dough on peel to bake on stone, dough and toppings can be divided in half and made, one at a time, into two 6″ to 8″ pizzas.)

Blot tomato slices dry and place them in a circle over pizza dough, covering it completely. Arrange mushroom slices over tomatoes and sprinkle with slivered olives. Drizzle evenly with the olive oil, garlic and oregano mixture. Bake in preheated oven until crust is lightly browned. Let stand at room temperature about 5 minutes before slicing and serving.

Makes one 12″ to 14″ round pizza or two 6″ to 8″ round pizzas.

● PIZZA PEPERONATA

Pizza becomes positively sensuous with this topping of braised sweet peppers, onions and tomatoes.

All-Purpose Pizza Dough for one
   12″ to 14″ round pizza (see
   Chapter 3)
Peperonata Topping (see recipe
   that follows)

¼ cup grated Parmesan cheese
3 thick slices Bel Paese cheese

Prepare pizza dough. Set aside to rise. While dough rises, prepare Peperonata Topping.

If baking pizza on preheated baking stone, place stone on center rack in oven and preheat oven to 450° F. If baking pizza in pizza pan, position oven rack on lowest level and preheat oven to 425° F.

When dough has risen, punch it down and turn it out on a lightly floured surface. Flatten out and shape as directed in pizza pan or on baker's peel. (If shaping dough on peel to bake on stone, dough and toppings can be divided in half and made, one at a time, into two 6″ to 8″ pizzas.)

Spread bottom of dough with Peperonata Topping. Sprinkle evenly with Parmesan cheese. Arrange Bel Paese slices in an attractive design over top.

Slide pizza from baker's peel onto preheated stone and reduce temperature to 425° F; or place pizza pan in oven. Bake about 20 minutes, until crust is lightly browned.

Let stand about 5 minutes at room temperature before slicing and serving.

Makes one 12″ to 14″ round pizza or two 6″ to 8″ round pizzas.

PEPERONATA TOPPING

2 tablespoons butter
2 tablespoons olive oil
1 lb. onions, peeled, very thinly
 sliced (about 4 cups)
1 lb. green bell peppers, seeded,
 thinly sliced
1 lb. red bell peppers, seeded,
 thinly sliced

1 28-oz. can Italian-style peeled
 tomatoes
1 tablespoon red wine vinegar
1 teaspoon sugar
1 teaspoon salt
Freshly ground black pepper

In a large, heavy skillet over medium heat, combine butter and olive oil. Add onions and cook, turning frequently, until soft and golden in color. Add peppers; reduce heat, cover and cook for about 10 minutes. Drain off about half of liquid from tomatoes (reserve for other use). Add tomatoes and remaining juice to skillet. Stir in vinegar, sugar, salt and pepper to taste; cover and cook for another 5 minutes. Then uncover and cook over high heat, stirring gently, until almost all liquid has evaporated.

Makes sufficient topping for one 12" to 14" round pizza or one 10" x 15" oblong pizza.

● EGGPLANT PIZZA WITH ZUCCHINI AND CHEESE

A lusty blend of fresh Mediterranean-style vegetables and cheeses.

All-Purpose Pizza Dough for oblong pizza (see Chapter 3)
1 small eggplant (about 10 oz.)
1 medium zucchini

Salt
2 tablespoons olive oil
1 medium onion, peeled,
 chopped

1 clove garlic, minced

2 to 4 tablespoons additional olive oil (more if needed)

½ cup flour

1 1-lb. can Italian plum tomatoes, drained and chopped

4 oz. grated Parmesan cheese

3 oz. grated mozzarella cheese

Prepare dough for oblong pizza. Set aside to rise.

Peel and cut eggplant into ¾" cubes. Trim zucchini and cut into thin slices. Place each vegetable in a separate bowl; sprinkle generously with salt. Let vegetables stand about 30 minutes; then transfer each to a colander and rinse under cold water. Blot dry.

Place flour in a shallow bowl; add eggplant cubes and mix to coat with flour. Shake off excess. Set aside.

Pour 2 tablespoons oil in a large, heavy skillet over medium heat. When hot, add onions; sauté until transparent. Add garlic; cook and stir another minute. Transfer with slotted spoon to a bowl; set aside. Add about one more tablespoon oil to skillet. When hot, add zucchini and sauté only until tender. Remove to a separate bowl. Set aside. Add about 1 more tablespoon oil to skillet. When hot, add eggplant cubes about ¼ at a time and fry until lightly browned on all sides, adding more oil if needed. Add eggplant as it is fried to bowl with onions and garlic.

Preheat oven to 425° F.

When dough has risen, punch down and turn out onto a lightly floured board; pat out into an 8" x 12" rectangle. Place on a 10" x 15" jelly roll pan and, with floured hands, press out to cover bottom and sides of pan evenly. Cover dough with tomatoes. Sprinkle with half of the grated Parmesan cheese. Spread eggplant, onion and garlic mixture evenly over surface; sprinkle with remaining Parmesan. Over cheese, arrange zucchini slices in a pattern. Top with shredded mozzarella. Bake in preheated oven about 15 to 20 minutes, until crust browns.

Makes one 15" x 10" oblong pizza.

● EPICUREAN SALT-FREE PIZZA

Mellowed garlic, fragrant herbs and creamy salt-free Gouda cheese make salt superfluous in this richly flavored pizza.

Salt-Free Pizza Dough (see
   Chapter 3)
¼ cup olive oil
1 clove garlic, peeled, finely
   minced
1 tablespoon minced fresh basil
   or ½ teaspoon dried basil
1 tablespoon minced fresh rosemary or ¼ teaspoon dried
   rosemary

¼ teaspoon dried oregano
1 lb. salt-free Gouda (or other
   salt-free cheese), cut into
   small cubes
3 lb. sun-ripened tomatoes

Prepare pizza dough. While dough rises, prepare toppings.

Pour oil into a small skillet over low heat. Add garlic and cook until fragrant. Remove from heat and pour into a medium-size bowl. Add basil, rosemary, oregano and cheese cubes.

Plunge each tomato into a large pan of rapidly boiling water for a few seconds. Hold each under cold running water and slip off the skin. Cut each in half and squeeze out all juice and seeds; chop each half coarsely, and blot dry. Set aside.

If preparing pizzas on baking stone, place stone on center rack in oven and preheat oven to 450° F. If preparing pizza in pizza pan, place rack on lowest position in oven and preheat oven to 425° F.

When dough has risen, punch it down and turn it out on a lightly floured work surface. Divide in half. Working one at a time, flatten and shape each half in pizza pan or on baker's peel, as directed. (If shaping on peel to bake on stone, dough and toppings can be divided in quarters and made, one at a time, into four 6″ to 8″ pizzas.) Cover bottom of dough with half of chopped tomatoes. Drain oil from cheese mixture, reserving oil. Sprinkle half of cheese, herbs and garlic evenly over tomatoes; sprinkle with a little of the reserved oil.

Slide pizza from peel onto heated baking stone and reduce

65

oven temperature to 425° F; or place pizza pan in preheated oven.

Bake about 20 minutes until crust is lightly browned.

Remove from oven. Repeat with remaining dough and toppings for second pizza.

Makes two 12" to 14" round pizzas or four 6" to 8" round pizzas.

● CHEESE LOVERS' PAN PIZZA

Cheesy Pizza Dough
4½ cups all-purpose flour
1 tablespoon salt
⅓ cup warm water (105° to 110° F)
1 tablespoon sugar
1 package dry yeast
1 whole egg, room temperature
3 egg yolks, room temperature

½ cup olive or vegetable oil, room temperature, or ½ cup melted butter
⅓ cup additional lukewarm water (105° to 110° F)
Additional flour, as needed
½ cup grated Romano or Parmesan cheese

Creamy Pizza Sauce
4 tablespoons butter
3 tablespoons flour
1½ cups fat-free chicken broth, room temperature

6 oz. grated sharp cheddar cheese
2 tablespoons tomato paste
Salt to taste

Topping
4 medium tomatoes
1 green pepper, seeded, cut into narrow strips

Dough: Combine flour and salt in a large mixing bowl. Set aside. Pour ⅓ cup water into a medium-size bowl and stir in the sugar. Sprinkle surface with yeast, stir once, let stand until mixture is bubbly. Add whole egg and egg yolks; beat until blended. Stir in oil or butter and remaining warm water; add to flour-salt mixture; stir to a soft dough. Sprinkle with a little additional flour, then shape dough into a ball in bowl. Turn out on a lightly floured surface. Knead for 2 to 3 minutes then start adding cheese a little at a time, kneading until cheese is blended into dough and dough is smooth and elastic. Form into a ball; place in a lightly greased bowl. Cover with plastic wrap or a clean dish towel. Let stand in a warm, draft-free place until volume doubles. While dough rises, prepare sauce and topping.

Sauce: Melt butter in a large, heavy skillet over medium heat. When bubbly, stir in flour. Cook and stir to a smooth, fragrant paste. Remove skillet from heat; gradually add broth, stirring as added. When smooth, return skillet to low heat. Cook and stir until mixture begins to thicken. Stir in cheese and tomato paste. Season lightly with salt. Continue to stir until cheese is melted and mixture very thick. Remove from heat, cool slightly, then cover sauce with plastic wrap until ready to use.

Topping: Cut tomatoes into thick slices (reserve end pieces for other use). Place slices on paper towels to drain. Drop green pepper strips in a large pot of rapidly boiling water. Boil 1 minute, transfer to colander; place under cold running water to stop cooking process.

When dough has risen, turn out on a lightly floured surface. Divide in half. Shape one half and place in pizza pan (according to directions in Chapter 3). Set remaining dough aside.

Preheat oven to 425° F. Spoon half of cheese sauce evenly over dough. Top evenly with half of tomatoes and green pepper. Bake in preheated oven 20 minutes or until edges of dough are lightly browned. Remove from oven; let stand while preparing second pizza. (First pizza will remain hot until the second pizza is baked.)

Makes two 12″ to 14″ round pizzas.

● PIZZA BIANCA ALLA ROMANA

(*Pizza with Mozzarella and Anchovies*)

This Neapolitan pizza is made without tomatoes but with plenty of extra cheese and piquant anchovies.

All-Purpose Pizza Dough for one 12″ to 14″ round pizza (see Chapter 3)

1 lb. whole-milk mozzarella cheese

1 2-oz. can flat anchovy filets in olive oil

2 tablespoons minced fresh basil or ½ teaspoon dried basil

¼ cup grated Parmesan cheese

Prepare pizza dough. Set aside to rise. While dough rises, prepare topping.

Grate mozzarella cheese on the coarse side of a hand grater or chop into very small pieces. Place in a bowl and add oil from anchovy filets. Chop filets and add them to the bowl. Stir to blend; set aside.

If baking pizza on baking stone, place stone on center rack in oven and preheat oven to 450° F. If baking pizza in pizza pan, place rack on lowest position in oven and preheat oven to 425° F.

When dough has risen, punch down and turn out on a lightly floured surface. Flatten out and shape in pizza pan or on baker's peel. (If shaping on peel to bake on stone, dough and toppings can be divided in half and made, one at a time, into two 6″ to 8″ pizzas.)

Spread pizza dough evenly with mozzarella and anchovy mixture. Sprinkle evenly with basil and grated Parmesan cheese. Slide pizza from baker's peel onto hot baking stone and reduce oven temperature to 425° F; or place pizza pan in oven.

Bake about 20 minutes until crust is lightly browned.

Let stand at room temperature about 5 minutes before slicing.

Makes one 12″ to 14″ round pizza or two 6″ to 8″ round pizzas.

● PIZZA WITH TUNA AND ANCHOVIES

We like to prepare enough pizza dough for two 12" to 14" round pizzas, using half for this intensely flavored, colorful pizza, and half for a traditional Pizza Margherita.

All-Purpose Pizza Dough for one 12" to 14" round pizza (see Chapter 3)
1 2-oz. can anchovy filets in olive oil
1 onion, peeled, very thinly sliced, slices broken into rings
1 cup homemade tomato sauce or 1 8-oz. can tomato sauce
1 tablespoon minced fresh rosemary or ½ teaspoon dried rosemary
1 7-oz. can solid packed tuna

Prepare pizza dough. Set aside to rise. While dough rises, prepare topping.

Drain oil from anchovy filets into a small skillet. Set filets aside. Place skillet over low heat. Add onions to anchovy oil and cook, stirring frequently, until pale golden and limp. Drain off and discard oil. Add tomato sauce; stir until bubbly. Remove from heat. Break tuna into bite-size chunks and add to sauce. Set aside.

If baking pizza on preheated baking stone, place stone on center rack in oven and preheat oven to 450° F. If baking pizza in pizza pan, position rack on lowest level and preheat oven to 425° F.

When dough has risen, punch down and turn out on a lightly floured surface. Flatten and shape in pizza pan or on baker's peel. (If shaping on peel to bake on stone, dough and toppings can be divided, one at a time, into two 6" to 8" pizzas.)

Spread dough evenly with tomato sauce–tuna mixture. Arrange anchovy filets in an attractive design over top.

Slide pizza from baker's peel onto preheated stone, or place pizza pan in oven. Bake about 20 minutes until crust is lightly browned.

Let stand at room temperature about 5 minutes before slicing and serving.

Makes one 12″ to 14″ round pizza or two 6″ to 8″ round pizzas.

● PIZZA VENETIAN

All-Purpose Pizza Dough for one
   12″ to 14″ round pizza (see
   Chapter 3)
1 lb. ground beef
1 medium onion, peeled,
   chopped
½ small green pepper, seeded,
   chopped
1 1-lb. can Italian-style
   tomatoes, drained, chopped

¼ cup raisins
8 to 10 green pimiento-stuffed
   olives, thinly sliced
⅛ teaspoon cinnamon
⅛ teaspoon ground cloves
1 oz. slivered almonds
2 oz. blue cheese, crumbled

Prepare pizza dough. Set aside to rise. While dough rises, prepare filling and topping.

In a large, heavy skillet cook meat, breaking up with a fork until lightly browned. Add onion and green pepper; stir-fry just until tender. Add tomatoes, raisins, olives and seasonings; stir to blend, then cook, stirring, about 3 minutes. Spoon off and discard rendered fat. Set aside.

If baking pizza on preheated baking stone, place stone on center rack in oven and preheat oven to 450° F. If baking pizza in pizza pan, place rack on lowest position in oven and preheat oven to 425° F.

When dough has risen, punch down and turn out on a lightly floured surface; flatten and shape in pizza pan or on baker's peel. (If shaping on peel to bake on stone, dough and toppings can be divided in half and made, one at a time, into two 6″ to 8″ pizzas.) Spread bottom of dough with meat mixture. Sprinkle top with slivered almonds and crumbled cheese.

Slide pizza from peel onto heated baking stone and reduce oven temperature to 425° F, or place pizza in pan in preheated oven.

Bake about 20 minutes until crust is lightly browned.

Remove from oven; let cool about 5 minutes before cutting and serving.

Makes one 12" to 14" round pizza or two 6" to 8" pizzas.

● PAN PIZZA WITH BROCCOLI AND PROSCIUTTO

A pizza crust topped with emerald-green broccoli, flavorful prosciutto and tomato sauce, then covered with creamy whole-milk mozzarella.

All-Purpose Pizza Dough for one
    12" to 14" round pizza (see
    Chapter 3)
1 10-oz. package frozen
    chopped broccoli or 1½ cups
    fresh broccoli flowerets,
    chopped
1 small green pepper
2 tablespoons olive oil
1 large onion, peeled, thinly
    sliced, slices broken into
    rings

2 cloves garlic, minced
1 cup homemade pizza sauce or
    1 8-oz. can pizza sauce
4 oz. prosciutto, thinly sliced,
    slices cut into narrow strips,
    or substitute Westphalian or
    Smithfield ham
1 cup shredded whole-milk
    mozzarella cheese (about 4
    oz.)

Prepare dough for pizza. Set aside to rise. While dough rises, prepare filling and toppings.

Cook frozen broccoli according to package directions or cook fresh broccoli in water until crisp-tender. Drain and set aside.

Cut ends from green pepper and set aside for other use. Cut remaining pepper across into thin rings; remove and discard seeds and tough white rims. Bring a large pot of water to full boil. Add green pepper rings; boil for 1 minute, then immediately drain into a colander and rinse with cold running water to stop cooking process. Set aside. Pour oil into large, heavy skillet over medium heat. When hot, add onions and sauté until transparent. Add garlic; stir until onions and garlic are tender. Remove from heat; set aside.

Place rack on lowest position in oven. Preheat oven to 425° F.

When dough has risen, punch down and turn out on a lightly floured surface; shape in pizza pan. Spread pizza sauce over dough. Arrange broccoli and ham over sauce. Top with onion mixture. Sprinkle with mozzarella. Arrange green pepper rings in attractive design over top. Bake in preheated oven about 20 minutes until crust is a crisp golden brown.

Makes one 12" to 14" round pizza.

● GENO'S PIZZA WITH PORK

All-Purpose Pizza Dough for one 12" to 14" round pizza (see Chapter 3)
1 lb. lean, boneless pork
2 tablespoons olive or vegetable oil
1 large green pepper, seeded, chopped
1 large onion, peeled, chopped
2 cloves garlic, peeled, minced

2 tablespoons tomato paste
1/2 cup water
1/8 teaspoon marjoram
1/4 teaspoon salt
1/4 teaspoon coarsely ground black pepper
2 oz. grated Parmesan cheese
6 oz. shredded mozzarella cheese

Prepare pizza dough. Set aside to rise. While dough rises, prepare filling and topping.

Place pork in freezer until very firm but not frozen. With a sharp knife chop into 1/4" cubes.

Pour oil into a large, heavy skillet over medium heat. When

hot, add pork and stir-fry until lightly browned. Add green pepper, onion and garlic; cook, stirring, until vegetables are tender. Stir in tomato paste and water. Season with marjoram, salt and pepper. Reduce heat; simmer, stirring occasionally, until mixture is almost dry. Set aside until cool.

If baking pizza on baking stone, place stone on center rack in oven and preheat oven to 450° F. If baking pizza in pizza pan, place rack on lowest position in oven and preheat oven to 425° F.

When dough has risen, punch down and turn out on a lightly floured surface. Flatten out and shape in pizza pan or on baker's peel. (If shaping on peel to bake on stone, dough and toppings can be divided in half and made, one at a time, into two 6″ to 8″ pizzas.)

Spread meat mixture over dough. Sprinkle evenly with cheeses. Slide pizza from baker's peel onto hot baking stone and reduce oven temperature to 425° F; or place pizza pan in preheated oven.

Bake 15 to 20 minutes until crust is lightly browned. Let stand at room temperature about 5 minutes before slicing.

Makes one 12″ to 14″ round pizza or two 6″ to 8″ round pizzas.

● SAUERKRAUT PAN PIZZA WITH CRISP PORK

This hearty and satisfying pizza has a surprise filling of mellowed sauerkraut and crisp-cooked shredded pork.

All-Purpose Pizza Dough for one 12″ to 14″ round pizza (see Chapter 3)

1 lb. sauerkraut

1 tablespoon olive or vegetable oil

1 large onion, peeled, chopped
1½ to 2 cups shredded, leftover
   roast pork or 3 boned, cooked
   pork chops
1 teaspoon caraway seeds
3 oz. shredded mozzarella
   cheese

3 oz. shredded fontina cheese,
   or 3 ounces additional
   mozzarella
2 thin slices mozzarella or
   fontina cheese, cut into ¼"
   strips

Prepare pizza dough. Set aside to rise. While dough rises, prepare filling and topping.

Place sauerkraut in a colander, wash under cold running water, then soak in a large bowl of cold water for 5 to 10 minutes. Drain, squeeze by handfuls to extract excess water, then fluff up strands; set aside.

Pour oil into a heavy skillet over medium-high heat. When hot, add onion and pork. Cook and stir until onion is tender and pork is crisp. Transfer with slotted spoon to a colander; drain; set aside.

Position rack in center of oven and preheat oven to 425° F.

When dough has risen, turn out on a lightly floured surface. Shape and place in pizza pan or on baking stone.

Using a fork, transfer sauerkraut to pizza shell, spreading out evenly. Cover evenly with pork and onion mixture. Sprinkle with caraway seeds and shredded cheeses. Arrange cheese strips in a pattern over surface. Place in preheated oven and bake 15 to 20 minutes until crust is lightly browned.

Let pizza stand at room temperature about 5 minutes before cutting. Serve hot.

Makes one 12" to 14" round pizza.

● PIZZA AMERICANA

Italians may have invented pizza, but it took an American to perfect this main-course version. It's based on a thick, homemade tomato sauce, lavishly topped with meat, cheese, fresh mushrooms and green onions. This recipe makes two great big beautiful 12" pizzas, enough for 4 to 6 pizza lovers. Any leftovers may be frozen, to reappear later as a glorious snack or midnight feast.

All-Purpose Pizza Dough for two
   12" to 14" round pizzas (see
   Chapter 3)
Sauce

2 tablespoons oil
1 small green pepper, seeded,
   chopped
1 large onion, peeled, chopped
1 small clove garlic, peeled,
   minced
1 28-oz. can whole tomatoes
   and their juice

1 6-oz. can tomato paste
1 tablespoon red wine vinegar
2 teaspoons sugar
1 teaspoon dried oregano
$\frac{1}{2}$ teaspoon salt
$\frac{1}{4}$ teaspoon pepper

Toppings

1$\frac{1}{2}$ lb. ground beef
1 3$\frac{1}{2}$-oz. package thinly sliced
   pepperoni, cut into strips
8 to 10 Niçoise-style olives,
   pitted, cut into slivers
$\frac{1}{4}$ lb. large mushrooms,
   trimmed, thinly sliced

6 to 8 green onions, trimmed,
   cut across, including green
   parts
4 oz. shredded mozzarella
   cheese
$\frac{1}{4}$ cup grated Parmesan cheese

Prepare pizza dough. While dough rises, prepare sauce and toppings.

   Sauce: Pour oil into large, heavy skillet over medium-high heat. When oil is hot, add green pepper and onion; cook and stir until vegetables are tender. Stir in garlic and cook until fragrant. Add tomatoes and their juice. Cook, breaking tomatoes up with the tip of a spoon or spatula until heated. Stir in tomato paste. Add vinegar, sugar, oregano, salt and pepper. Bring to boil; reduce heat. Simmer, stirring occasionally, about 30 minutes until sauce is very thick. Set aside.

Toppings: Brown ground beef in a large, heavy skillet over medium-high heat, stirring to break up pieces. Drain off fat. Stir in basil and pepperoni strips. Add olives, mushrooms and green onion.

When dough has risen, turn out on a lightly floured surface. Divide in half. Shape one half and place in pizza pan. Set remaining dough aside.

Preheat oven to 425° F. When oven has reached desired temperature, spoon half of tomato sauce evenly over dough. Top evenly with half of ground beef mixture. Sprinkle with half of cheeses. Bake 15 to 20 minutes or until edges of dough are lightly browned. Remove from oven; let stand while preparing second pizza. (First pizza will remain hot until the second pizza is baked.)

Makes two 12" to 14" round pizzas.

● PIZZA AMERICANA WITH SHRIMP

This American pizza brings Italy to your table: its colors are intense, its flavors superb.

All-Purpose Pizza Dough for two 12″ to 14″ round pizzas (see Chapter 3)

1 1-lb. can Italian plum tomatoes, drained

2 cups homemade tomato sauce or 1 1-lb. can tomato sauce

1 6-oz. can tomato paste

1 cup water

½ cup slivered Sicilian cracked green olives

½ cup slivered Kalamata olives

1 lb. peeled, deveined, cooked shrimp, coarsely chopped

1 tablespoon olive oil

6 to 8 large mushrooms, coarsely chopped

1 clove garlic, peeled, minced

1 medium onion, peeled, coarsely chopped

1 small green pepper, seeded, thinly sliced

1 teaspoon ground oregano

4 oz. shredded mozzarella cheese

4 oz. shredded provolone cheese

2 oz. grated Parmesan cheese

Prepare pizza dough. Set aside to rise. While dough rises, prepare sauce and topping.

In a large, heavy saucepan, combine tomatoes, tomato sauce, tomato paste and water. Cook, breaking up tomatoes with the tip of a spoon and stirring frequently, for 5 to 10 minutes or until sauce thickens. Remove from heat. When cool, stir in olives and shrimp.

Pour oil into a second skillet over low heat. Add mushrooms, garlic, onion and green pepper. Cook, stirring, until vegetables are crisp-tender. Set aside.

When dough has risen, turn out on a lightly floured surface. Divide in half. Shape one half and place in pizza pan. Set remaining dough aside.

Preheat oven to 425° F.

Spoon half of tomato sauce and shrimp mixture evenly over surface. Cover with half of the sautéed vegetable mixture. Sprinkle with half of cheeses. Bake in preheated oven 15 to

77

20 minutes, or until edges of dough are lightly browned. Remove from oven; let stand while preparing second pizza with remaining ingredients. (First pizza will remain hot until second is baked.)

Makes two 12″ to 14″ round pizzas.

● SICILIAN-STYLE PIZZA

The dough for Sicilian-style pizza is shaped in an oblong pan, then allowed to rise in the pan again. The result is a crust that is light yet hearty and flavorful.

SICILIAN-STYLE PIZZA DOUGH

¼ cup warm water (105° to 110° F)

1 package dry yeast

1 teaspoon sugar

1 cup additional warm water (105° to 110° F)

1 cup unbleached all-purpose flour

1½ teaspoons salt

2 tablespoons olive oil

2 cups additional unbleached all-purpose flour

½ cup whole wheat flour

Additional flour, as needed

Pour ¼ cup warm water into a large mixing bowl. Sprinkle yeast and sugar over surface. Stir once and let stand until yeast has dissolved and mixture is bubbly. Stir in remaining water. Add 1 cup all-purpose flour, salt and oil. Beat to a smooth batter. Stir in remaining flour to form a dough sufficiently firm to pull loose and hold its shape in bowl, adding additional flour if necessary. Turn out on a lightly floured surface. Knead until smooth and elastic, adding more flour as needed to keep dough from sticking to work surface. Form into a ball, place in a lightly greased bowl and turn to grease all sides. Cover bowl with plastic wrap or clean dish towel. Let stand in a warm, draft-free place until volume doubles. Punch down and knead about 1 minute in bowl. Cover and let rise a second time.

78

Transfer dough from bowl to floured work surface. Flatten with floured hands into a rectangle about 6" × 12".

Lightly grease a 9" x 15" x 2" baking pan. Place rectangle of dough in pan and press out to cover bottom and form a slight rim. Cover pan. Let stand about 30 minutes.

Preheat oven to 425° F.

Cover dough with sauce and topping. Bake 25 to 30 minutes or until crust is lightly browned.

Makes one 9" x 15" oblong pizza.

MARIA'S SICILIAN-STYLE PIZZA WITH EGGPLANT

This glorious pizza is filled with eggplant, tomato sauce, a variety of cheeses and olives. It's not just a meal, it's a feast.

Sicilian-Style Pizza Dough
1 medium eggplant
Salt
Olive or vegetable oil, about 3 tablespoons
1½ cups homemade tomato sauce, or 1½ cups canned tomato sauce
4 oz. mozzarella cheese cut into thin, narrow strips
2 tablespoons grated Parmesan cheese

½ teaspoon oregano
¼ teaspoon basil
15 oz. ricotta cheese
1½ cups additional tomato sauce
4 oz. shredded mozzarella cheese
2 tablespoons additional grated Parmesan cheese
8 to 12 large imported Spanish green olives, seeded, sliced

Prepare pizza dough. While dough rises in pan, prepare sauce and toppings.

Peel eggplant and cut into ¼" slices. Sprinkle each slice lightly with salt on both sides. Place in stacks of three on a double thickness of paper towels. Cover stacks with a long, wooden chopping board, or with heavy plates. Let stand about 30 minutes to drain. Rinse slices under cold, running water and blot thoroughly dry.

Pour oil into large, heavy skillet over medium heat. When hot, fry eggplant slices a few at a time until tender, adding additional oil if needed. Blot slices dry with paper towels. Set aside.

Preheat oven to 450° F.

When dough has risen in pan, spread 1½ cups tomato sauce evenly over surface. Bake in preheated oven for 10 minutes. Remove from oven and top with eggplant slices. Cover with mozzarella slices and sprinkle with two tablespoons Parmesan cheese, the oregano and basil. Spoon ricotta cheese evenly over surface. Top with remaining tomato sauce, shredded mozzarella, Parmesan cheese and olives.

Return pizza to oven and bake 20 to 25 minutes or until crust is lightly browned, cheese has melted and filling is bubbly hot.

Let stand at room temperature about 10 minutes before cutting and serving.

Makes one 9″ x 15″ oblong pizza.

SICILIAN-STYLE PIZZA WITH CAPONATA

Sicilian-Style Pizza Dough
¼ cup olive oil or mild
   vegetable oil
1 medium onion, peeled,
   chopped
1 small green pepper, seeded,
   cut into narrow strips
½ cup thinly sliced celery
1 small eggplant, trimmed, cut
   into ¼″ cubes
1 small zucchini, trimmed, cut
   into ½″ cubes

1 1-lb. can Italian-style tomato
   sauce with basil
1 tablespoon red wine vinegar
1 teaspoon sugar
Coarsely ground black pepper
   to taste
Salt to taste (optional)
½ lb. mozzarella cheese, cut
   into thin strips

Prepare pizza dough. While dough rises the second time, prepare filling and topping.

Pour oil into a large, heavy skillet over medium heat. When hot, add onion, green pepper, celery, eggplant and zucchini. Cook, stirring frequently, for about 10 minutes or until vegetables are crisp-tender. Pour in tomato sauce. Add vinegar and sugar. Season with pepper and, if desired, salt. Stir to blend. Simmer uncovered for about 10 minutes. Set aside to cool for at least 10 minutes or until dough has risen and is ready to shape.

Preheat oven to 425° F.

When dough has risen, punch down and shape in pan as directed. Set aside in pan to rise 30 minutes. Spoon in caponata filling. Arrange cheese over surface. Bake 15 to 20 minutes, until crust is lightly browned.

Let stand at room temperature about 5 minutes before cutting. Serve hot.

Makes one 10" x 15" oblong pizza.

SICILIAN-STYLE PIZZA WITH SAUSAGE

Some things in this world cannot be improved. This Sicilian interpretation of pizza is perfection.

Sicilian-Style Pizza Dough
4 Italian-style pork sausage
   links (about ¼ lb.)
Water
1 tablespoon olive oil
2 onions, peeled, chopped
1 small green pepper, seeded,
   chopped
1 1-lb. can Italian-style peeled
   tomatoes and their juice
1 6-oz. can tomato paste
2 tomato paste cans of water

¼ teaspoon dried basil
¼ teaspoon dried oregano
¼ teaspoon dried thyme
½ teaspoon salt
Black pepper to taste
Sprinkling of hot pepper flakes
4 oz. mozzarella cheese,
   coarsely chopped
¼ cup black Sicilian olives,
   slivered

Prepare pizza dough. While dough is rising the second time, prepare sausage, sauce and toppings.

Prick each sausage in several places with the tip of a knife. Place in a small saucepan. Cover them about halfway with water. Bring to boil, lower heat and simmer until water evaporates completely. Cook, turning frequently, until links are browned on all sides. Remove sausages from skillet with slotted spoon; cool slightly, then cut into ¼" slices. Set aside.

Add olive oil to rendered sausage fat in skillet. Place over medium heat. Add onions and green pepper. Cook, stirring, about 10 minutes until vegetables are tender. Pour in tomatoes and their juice. Cook, breaking up tomatoes with tip of a wooden spoon or a spatula until mixture comes to a boil. Stir in tomato paste and water. Add herbs, salt, pepper and hot pepper flakes. Cook over medium heat, stirring often, about 30 minutes until sauce is very thick. Set aside.

When dough has risen, turn out on a lightly floured surface; shape and place in oblong pan. Set aside to rise in pan for 30 minutes.

Preheat oven to 425° F.

When oven has reached desired temperature, spoon tomato sauce evenly over dough. Top evenly with sausage slices, chopped cheese and olives. Bake 15 to 20 minutes, or until edges of dough are lightly browned. Let stand at room temperature about 5 minutes before slicing.

Makes one 9" x 15" oblong pizza.

● SOUTH-OF-THE-BORDER-STYLE PIZZA

A different pizza crust made with Mexican cornmeal and topped with favorite taco ingredients. The method is Italian, the flavoring is Mexican, the blend is explosive. You'll love it!

MEXICAN PIZZA DOUGH

2½ cups all-purpose flour
½ cup Masa Harina meal* or finely ground yellow corn meal
1 package dry yeast

1 teaspoon sugar
1 teaspoon salt
1 cup water
2 tablespoons oil

*Masa Harina is a finely ground corn meal that has been treated with lime. It is sold by the Quaker Oats Company and is available in health food stores, gourmet shops and many supermarkets.

In a large bowl, combine 1 cup flour, the Masa Harina meal or corn meal, yeast, sugar and salt; mix well. In a saucepan heat water and oil until lukewarm (105° to 110° F); stir into flour-yeast mixture. Gradually stir in one cup of the remaining flour to make a soft dough. Turn out on a lightly floured surface. Sprinkle top of dough lightly with some of the remaining flour; knead until smooth and elastic, adding flour if needed to keep dough from sticking. Form into a ball and place in a lightly greased bowl. Turn to coat dough completely with oil. Cover bowl with plastic wrap. Let dough rise in a warm draft-free place about 1 hour until light and double in bulk.

Makes sufficient dough for one 12″ to 14″ round pizza.

MEXICAN PIZZA

Mexican Pizza Dough
1 lb. lean ground beef
1 large onion, peeled, chopped
1 large clove garlic, peeled, minced
1 teaspoon dried oregano
2 teaspoons chili powder (or to taste)
1 teaspoon ground cumin (optional)

Salt and freshly ground black pepper, to taste
1 1-lb. can tomato sauce
1 4-oz. can chopped jalapeño peppers, drained
½ lb. sliced Monterey Jack cheese, slices cut into ¼″ strips
1 small onion, peeled, finely chopped

Prepare Mexican Pizza Dough. Set aside to rise. While dough rises, prepare filling and toppings.

Place a large skillet over medium heat; add beef and cook, stirring to break up pieces, until browned. Drain off fat. Add onions and garlic. Cook, stirring, about 1 minute. Stir in oregano, chili powder and, if desired, cumin. Season to taste with salt and pepper. Add tomato sauce and jalapeño peppers; stir. Reduce heat, and simmer gently for about 15 minutes or until sauce is thick. Remove from heat to cool. Set aside at room temperature until ready to use.

Preheat oven to 425° F.

When dough has risen, punch down and turn out on a

lightly floured surface. Form into a ball. Place ball on a lightly greased 12″ to 14″ pizza pan or on a baking stone. Using the palms of your hands, pat dough into pizza pan and press out to cover bottom and sides of pan completely, or press out on baking stone; turn edges of dough inward and press up to form rim. Spread sauce mixture over dough to edge. Top with cheese strips. Bake in preheated oven 15 to 20 minutes. Set aside to keep warm. Sprinkle pizza with chopped onions just before serving.

Makes one 12″ to 14″ round pizza.

MEXICAN PIZZA WITH SAUSAGE AND PEPPERS

Mexican Pizza Dough
1 lb. bulk sausage meat, highly
  seasoned or mild
2 4-oz. cans taco sauce
¼-oz. can chopped jalapeño
  peppers, drained

¼ lb. fontina cheese, finely
  diced
¼ lb. mozzarella cheese,
  coarsely shredded

Prepare Mexican Pizza Dough. Set aside to rise. While dough rises, prepare filling and toppings.

In a large, heavy skillet over medium heat cook sausage meat, stirring to break up pieces, until well browned. Drain off fat. Add taco sauce and jalapeño peppers. Cook and stir until sauce is bubbly hot. Remove from heat. Set aside until cool.

Preheat oven to 425° F.

When dough has risen, punch down and turn out on a lightly floured surface; pat out into an 8″ x 12″ rectangle. Place on a 10″ x 15″ jelly roll pan and with floured hands press out to cover bottom and sides of pan evenly. Spread sausage mixture evenly over dough. Sprinkle evenly with cheeses.

Bake in preheated oven until crust is lightly browned.

Makes one 10″ x 15″ inch oblong pizza.

●COUNTRY PIE-PAN PIZZA

In Italian pizza simply means pie, but in Italy pie is never just simple. This Piedmont-style creation is proof.

Rich Pizza Crust (see recipe
  that follows)
1 10-oz. package frozen,
  chopped spinach
1 cup ricotta cheese (1 8-oz.
  container)
3/4 cup shredded mozzarella
  cheese

2 tablespoons freshly grated
  Romano or Parmesan cheese
1/4 lb. Italian salami, chopped
1 egg, lightly beaten
1/8 teaspoon marjoram
1/4 teaspoon oregano
1/2 teaspoon salt
1/8 teaspoon pepper

Prepare bottom and top crusts for baking. Refrigerate until ready to fill.

Place spinach in a colander until completely thawed. (To hasten thawing, place colander under hot running water until spinach can be broken into large chunks, then work with your hands until completely thawed.) Pick thawed spinach up in your hands and squeeze until thoroughly dry.

Preheat oven to 425° F.

In a large bowl, combine thawed spinach, ricotta, mozzarella and Romano or Parmesan cheeses. Stir in chopped salami, egg, marjoram, oregano, salt and pepper. Blend mixture thoroughly. Spoon into prepared bottom crust. Arrange top crust over filling. Trim edges 1/2" larger than pan, turn under and flute. Brush top with cold water. Cut small slits in center of top crust in several places. Place in preheated oven and bake about 30 minutes until filling bubbles up and crust is deep golden brown.

Makes one 9" pie pizza.

RICH PIZZA CRUST

2 cups all-purpose flour
1 teaspoon salt
⅓ cup lard or vegetable
  shortening
4 tablespoons chilled butter
  (½ stick)

2 tablespoons fresh strained
  lemon juice
2 to 3 tablespoons ice water
Additional flour as needed

Combine flour and salt in a large bowl. Cut in lard or shortening with a pastry blender, two knives or your fingers until mixture resembles coarse meal.

Cut chilled butter in half lengthwise, then cut across into ¼" pieces and add to bowl. Work into flour mixture until evenly distributed in chunks about the size of small green peas. Sprinkle surface with lemon juice and about 2 tablespoons chilled water. With a fork, toss lightly until mixture comes together, adding 1 tablespoon water if needed. Form dough into a ball. Wrap loosely in waxed paper or leave ball in bowl and cover with plastic wrap. Refrigerate until chilled or until ready to roll out.

Divide chilled dough in half and roll one half out on a lightly floured surface into an 11" circle; fit into a 9" pie pan. Roll remaining dough into a 12" circle for top of pie; place on foil or a flat baking sheet. Refrigerate shaped dough in pan and rolled out top crust while preparing filling.

● COUNTRY PIZZA

A double-crust pizza pie with chopped broccoli and four cheeses. No tomatoes!

Country Pizza Crust (see recipe that follows)

1 10-oz. package frozen chopped broccoli, cooked, drained

1 cup ricotta cheese (1 8-oz. container)

½ cup shredded mozzarella cheese

¼ cup slivered provolone cheese

2 tablespoons grated Parmesan cheese

¼ lb. thinly sliced pepperoni, cut into slivers

1 egg, lightly beaten

½ teaspoon salt

¼ teaspoon dried rosemary

¼ teaspoon dried oregano

Prepare pizza crust.

Preheat oven to 375° F.

In a large bowl, combine broccoli, ricotta, mozzarella, provolone and Parmesan cheese. Stir in pepperoni and beaten egg. Season with salt, rosemary and oregano. Spoon mixture into prepared crust. Cover with top crust. Bring edges of bottom crust over top crust and pinch together to form rim. Brush top crust lightly with water, and with a small knife cut two crisscross slashes in center. Bake in preheated oven 45 minutes to 1 hour or until crust is light golden brown.

Makes one 9″ pie pizza.

COUNTRY PIZZA CRUST

2 cups all-purpose flour

½ teaspoon salt

¼ cup butter

½ cup vegetable shortening

Approximately 6 tablespoons cold water

Combine flour and salt in a medium-size bowl. With a pastry blender, two knives or your fingers, cut in butter and shortening until mixture resembles coarse meal. Sprinkle cold water evenly over surface. Stir with a fork until dough clings together and leaves sides of bowl. Turn out onto a floured surface. Divide in half and form each half into a ball. One at a time, roll out each ball on floured surface into a 12" circle, turning dough often and sprinkling lightly with flour to prevent sticking. Fold rolled dough in half and then in quarters. Center quarter in a 9" pie pan and gently unfold. Without stretching, press dough evenly up sides of pan. Trim overlapping pastry evenly with edge of pan. Refrigerate until ready to use. Roll second ball of pastry in the same way. Place on flat surface and refrigerate until ready to use.

• DEEP-DISH "CHICAGO-STYLE PIZZA"

A festive, double-crusted, double-garnished, double-delicious pizza that's a positive celebration of life.

½ cup warm water (105° to 110° F)

2 teaspoons sugar

1 package dry yeast

1½ cups all-purpose flour

1½ teaspoons salt

1 cup additional warm water (105° to 110° F)

¼ cup olive oil, room temperature

2½ cups additional all-purpose flour

Additional flour, as needed

Desired filling (see recipes that follow)

1 cup homemade pizza or tomato sauce, or 1 8-oz. can pizza or tomato sauce

1 cup shredded mozzarella cheese

½ cup grated Parmesan cheese

Pour ½ cup water into a large bowl. Add sugar and yeast. Stir once, then let stand about 5 minutes until bubbly. Add 1½ cups flour, salt, 1 cup warm water and oil. Blend thoroughly. Stir in remaining flour to form a stiff dough. Turn out on a lightly floured surface and knead about 8 minutes until smooth and elastic, adding additional flour if needed to keep dough from sticking. Form into a ball, place in a lightly greased bowl, turning to coat all sides. Cover bowl with plastic wrap or clean dish towel and place in a warm, draft-free place about 1½ hours until volume doubles.

While dough rises, prepare filling.

Preheat oven to 450° F.

When dough has risen, punch down and turn out on a lightly floured surface. Cut off one third and set aside. Roll out remaining dough to a 20″ circle, then roll it loosely over rolling pin, lift and unroll carefully over pizza pan. Lift edges of dough and let it fall gently into place, patting it lightly into the bottom and up sides of pan without forcing or stretching. Spoon in desired filling.

Roll out remaining dough to a circle about 14″ in diameter. Roll loosely over pin, lift, then unroll carefully over filling. Fold bottom dough inward and crimp with top dough to form a raised rim. Bake in preheated oven 18 to 20 minutes or until crust is lightly browned. Remove from oven. If desired, set aside at room temperature for 2 to 3 hours.

Spoon tomato sauce over crust and top with cheeses. Return pizza to oven and continue to bake until cheese is melted and sauce bubbly hot. Let stand at room temperature about 10 minutes before serving.

Makes one 14″ deep-dish pizza (8 to 10 servings).

VITO'S FILLING WITH MEATBALLS

Meatballs (see recipe that follows) or Meatballs with Parmesan cheese (see Chapter 4)

2 tablespoons olive oil

1 large onion, peeled, coarsely chopped

2 large green peppers, seeded, cut into ½″ cubes

2 cups homemade tomato sauce, or 2 1-lb. cans tomato sauce

2 tablespoons grated Parmesan cheese

Prepare meatballs.

Pour oil into a large, heavy skillet over medium-high heat. When hot, add onion and green pepper. Cook, stirring, until vegetables are tender. Pour in tomato sauce; bring to simmer. Add meatballs. Lower heat and leave to simmer for 20 to 25 minutes. Stir in grated cheese; cook, stirring, until sauce is very thick. Set aside at room temperature until ready to use.

MEATBALLS

1 cup fresh white-bread crumbs	¼ teaspoon coarsely ground
3 tablespoons dry red wine	black pepper
1 lb. lean pork, such as pork	¼ teaspoon dried rosemary
shoulder	¼ teaspoon dried basil
1 lb. fatty pork butt	¼ teaspoon dried oregano
1 teaspoon salt	2 eggs

Place bread crumbs in a small bowl; stir in wine. Set aside.

Place meat in freezer until very firm but not frozen; cut into small cubes.

Grind meat and fat together, first coarsely and then finely; or place in work bowl of food processor and process until finely ground. Transfer to a large bowl. Add salt, pepper, rosemary, basil, oregano, eggs and softened bread crumbs. Mix with your hands until thoroughly blended.

Cover and refrigerate for 1 to 4 hours to blend flavors.

Form mixture into 1″ balls.

Preheat oven to 425° F.

Arrange meatballs in single layer in roasting pan. Bake in preheated oven, turning occasionally, until lightly browned. Transfer with slotted spoon to paper towels to drain. Set aside until ready to use; or place in single layer on a long, flat baking sheet in freezer until very firm and then store in airtight container in freezer up to 2 weeks.

Makes about 20 meatballs.

SAUSAGE AND BROCCOLI FILLING

1 bunch broccoli, enough to
make about 6 cups coarsely
chopped broccoli
1 lb. Smithfield bulk sausage
meat
1 medium onion, peeled,
chopped
1 clove garlic, peeled, minced

2 tablespoons grated Parmesan
or Romano cheese
1 cup homemade pizza or
tomato sauce, or 1 8-oz. can
pizza or tomato sauce
½ cup sliced pimiento-stuffed
green olives

Cut broccoli tops from stems. Break tops into flowerets. Trim
and coarsely chop stems. Rinse under cold running water.
Place on rack in steamer pot over simmering water; steam only
until crisp-tender. Set aside.

In a large, heavy skillet over medium heat, cook sausage,
stirring frequently and breaking meat up with a fork until
browned. Add onion and garlic; cook until tender. Scrape contents of skillet into a colander; drain. Transfer to a large bowl.
Stir in broccoli, cheese, sauce and olives. Set aside until ready
to use.

● CALZONE

---

*A calzone is an extraordinary, extravagant turnover, larger
than Neapolitan life and just as exciting. It is made with a
glorious yeasty dough and filled with your favorite pizza
ingredients.*

*Until just a few years ago calzone was so unknown in
America that any Italian restaurant serving it was described
as a place where you could "order something you've never
eaten before."*

All-Purpose Pizza Dough for one
12" to 14" round pizza (see
Chapter 3)

Desired filling (see recipes that
follow)

Prepare pizza dough. Set aside to rise. While dough rises, prepare filling.

Preheat oven to 425° F.

When dough has risen, turn out on a lightly floured surface. Punch down, shape into a 12″ oval, following basic pizza dough directions for home-style pizza. (Calzone is formed in an oval instead of circle so filling will fit in corners when dough is folded over.) Place flat baking sheet lengthwise in front of you; arrange half of long side of dough on center of sheet, leaving other half overlapping sheet. Pile desired filling on half of dough, leaving ½″ border. Brush edges of dough with water. Fold other half of dough over to form turnover, pressing edges together with fingers; use a fork to flute edges decoratively. With the tip of a knife, make three steam vents in top of turnover. Place in preheated oven and bake 15 minutes; lower heat to 350° F and bake another 15 minutes. If dough becomes too brown, cover with foil for last 10 minutes. Remove from oven and let calzone stand at room temperature for about 5 minutes before cutting. Serve warm.

Serves 4.

RICOTTA FILLING FOR CALZONE

This mellow but flavorful filling is perfect for a calzone appetizer. Serve warm or at room temperature, cut across into slices.

1 cup ricotta cheese, drained if necessary
1 egg yolk
2 tablespoons grated Parmesan cheese
½ cup slivered, extra-sharp, imported provolone cheese

2 tablespoons slivered black olives; or 2 to 3 anchovy filets, drained, blotted dry, cut across into thin slivers

In a bowl, mash ricotta with egg yolk until blended and smooth. Stir in remaining ingredients.

Makes sufficient filling for one large or two small calzones.

PESTO AND RICOTTA FILLING FOR CALZONE

½ cup fresh basil leaves, washed, drained and tightly packed; or ½ cup finely chopped parsley leaves, plus 2 teaspoons dried basil

2 tablespoons olive oil
2 teaspoons salt
1 1-lb. container ricotta cheese, drained
¼ cup grated Parmesan cheese

Place all ingredients in container of a food processor or blender and process or blend, stirring down with rubber spatula as necessary, until mixture is smooth. Set aside until ready to use.

Makes sufficient filling for one large or two small calzones.

BEEF AND CHEESE FILLING FOR CALZONE

1 lb. ground beef
1 medium onion, peeled, chopped
1 clove garlic, peeled, minced
4 tablespoons tomato paste
4 tablespoons dry white wine
2 oz. Chèvre cheese, coarsely chopped; or herb-seasoned Boursin

2 to 3 tablespoons ricotta cheese
1 egg yolk, lightly beaten
Salt to taste
Coarsely ground black pepper to taste

In a large, heavy skillet over medium heat cook beef until no longer pink. Add onion and garlic; stir until tender. Tilt skillet,

93

and spoon off rendered fat. Stir in tomato paste and wine. Cook, stirring, until mixture is very thick. Remove from heat, cool to room temperature. Stir in cheeses and egg yolk. Blend well. Season lightly with salt, heavily with pepper. Set aside until ready to use.

Makes sufficient filling for one large or two small calzones.

CHEESE AND PROSCIUTTO FILLING FOR CALZONE

3 to 4 oz. soft, creamy Chèvre cheese

1 to 2 tablespoons half-and-half or milk (optional)

1 cup ricotta cheese

4 oz. fontina cheese, chopped

2 oz. prosciutto, minced (about ½ cup); or other dried, cured ham, thinly sliced and chopped

½ teaspoon dried basil and/or oregano

In a large bowl, mash Chèvre with a fork, adding cream or milk if it is too dry. Add ricotta. Stir in fontina and prosciutto. Season with herbs. Blend well. Set aside until ready to use.

Makes sufficient filling for one large or two small calzones.

PICNIC FILLING FOR CALZONE

6 oz. diced mozzarella cheese

2 oz. prosciutto, cut into slivers

2 oz. Genoa salami, finely chopped

¼ cup grated Parmesan cheese

Pinch of basil

6 to 8 large mushrooms, trimmed, chopped

1 egg, lightly beaten

In a bowl, combine ingredients. Blend well.

Makes sufficient filling for one large or two small calzones.

● SFINCIUNI

(Palermo-Style Stuffed Pizza)

Sfinciuni are for pizza lovers who claim they like the crust even better than the topping. The first layer of dough is covered with sauce and topping, then covered with a second layer of dough before it is baked, transforming the topping into a glorious filling.

All-Purpose Pizza Dough, for one 12″ to 14″ pizza (see Chapter 3)

Desired filling (see recipes that follow)

Prepare pizza dough. Set aside to rise.

While dough rises, prepare desired filling; set aside until ready to use.

Place a baking stone on uppermost rack in oven. Preheat oven to 450° F.

When dough has risen, punch down and turn out on a lightly floured surface; divide in half. Flatten one half into a disk. Place on a lightly floured baker's peel or a sheet of heavy-duty cardboard and flatten out into a circle about 8″ in diameter. Spoon desiring filling evenly over dough, leaving about ½″ uncovered rim.

Flatten out remaining ball of dough until just large enough to cover the first. Place over the filling, roll bottom round of dough up over top dough and pinch together to form a tight seal.

Slide the filled dough on to the preheated baking stone. Reduce oven temperature to 425° F. Bake for 15 to 20 minutes or until crust is lightly browned. To allow flavors of the filling to develop, let the pizza stand at room temperature 15 to 20 minutes before slicing.

Makes one 8″ double-crust stuffed pizza.

WINTER VEGETABLE FILLING

1 10-oz. package frozen,
  chopped broccoli
¼ lb. thinly sliced, smoked
  ham with some fat
2 tablespoons butter
1 medium onion, peeled, finely
  chopped
⅓ cup raisins
¼ cup dry, white wine or
  vermouth

1 12-oz. package cream cheese,
  room temperature
2 egg yolks
½ cup coarsely chopped
  walnuts
⅛ teaspoon dried rosemary
¼ teaspoon salt
Pepper to taste
4 oz. Gruyère cheese, coarsely
  chopped

Cook broccoli according to package directions. Drain. Set aside.

Trim fat from ham. Dice fat; cut meat into 2″ squares. Set aside.

Melt butter in a large, heavy skillet over medium heat. Add diced ham fat; cook, stirring, until crisp. Add ham and stir about 30 seconds. Stir in onion. Add raisins, broccoli and wine or vermouth. Set aside to cool.

In a large mixing bowl, combine cream cheese and egg yolks; beat until smooth. Add walnuts, rosemary and broccoli mixture. Season with salt and pepper. Blend well. Cool to room temperature. Add Gruyère cheese. Set aside until ready to use.

SPINACH AND MUSHROOM FILLING

1 10-oz. package frozen
  chopped spinach
2 tablespoons olive oil
¼ lb. mushrooms, trimmed,
  coarsely chopped
2 tablespoons finely chopped
  shallots or green onions

¼ cup dry white wine
¼ cup chopped mild salami
½ cup finely diced fontina
  cheese
2 tablespoons packaged Italian-
  seasoned bread crumbs
½ teaspoon mixed Italian herbs

Cook spinach according to package directions. Drain. Set aside.

Pour oil into a large, heavy skillet over medium heat. When hot, add mushrooms and shallots; sauté until shallots are transparent, mushrooms crisp-tender. Tilt pan and spoon off oil. Add spinach and wine. Increase heat to high and cook, stirring, until wine has evaporated and mixture is dry. Transfer to a mixing bowl. Cool to room temperature. Stir in salami, fontina cheese, bread crumbs and Italian herbs. Set aside until ready to use.

SAUSAGE AND CHEESE FILLING

1 lb. fresh bulk Italian-style sausage
2 tablespoons olive oil
1 small onion, peeled, minced
1 small clove garlic, peeled, minced
1 1-lb. can Italian-style tomatoes and their juice
½ teaspoon coarsely ground black pepper
½ teaspoon oregano
½ teaspoon basil
½ teaspoon salt
2 tablespoons heavy cream
¾ cup finely diced mozzarella cheese (about 4 oz.)
¼ cup freshly grated Parmesan cheese

In a large, heavy skillet over medium heat, fry the sausage, breaking it up as it cooks, about 15 minutes until browned. Transfer to colander to drain. Set aside. Wipe skillet clean with paper toweling. Add the oil and place over medium heat. When oil is hot, add onion and garlic; sauté about 3 minutes until transparent. Add tomatoes and their juice, pepper, oregano, basil and salt. Stir in sausage. Lower heat and let simmer for about 15 minutes, stirring often. Stir in cream. Cook and stir until sauce thickens. Let cool to room temperature. Stir in cheeses. Set aside until ready to use.

● TOP-OF-THE-STOVE PIZZAS

Would you believe it? Pizza cooked in a skillet on top of the stove, outdoors on your barbeque grill or even over a campfire (for those times when the fish don't bite).

All-Purpose Pizza Dough for one
   12″ to 14″ round pizza (see
   Chapter 3)
Desired topping and cheese (see
   recipes that follow)

Approximately 6 tablespoons
   olive oil

Prepare pizza dough. Set aside to rise. While dough rises prepare topping: set aside.

When dough has risen, punch down and turn out on a lightly floured surface. Separate into 6 equal parts. Stretch and flatten one part, as directed, into a 7″ to 8″ circle.

Pour about 1 tablespoon of oil into a 10″ skillet. Place over high heat. When hot, place circle of dough in skillet and immediately reduce heat to medium. Fry for about 5 minutes or until bottom side is lightly browned. Turn dough over. Cover skillet and let pizza cook about 10 minutes. Cover with desired topping to about ½″ of rim. Sprinkle with desired cheese. Re-cover skillet and continue to cook until topping is hot and cheese has melted. Transfer pizza to a warm oven. Repeat with remaining oil, dough, topping and cheese.

Makes six 6″ to 7″ pizzas.

ZUCCHINI TOPPING WITH MOZZARELLA

2 tablespoons olive oil
1 small onion, peeled, minced
1 medium clove garlic, peeled, minced
3 or 4 small to medium zucchini, trimmed, thinly sliced
4 tablespoons tomato paste

2 tablespoons water
1/2 teaspoon oregano
1/4 teaspoon basil
Salt to taste
Coarsely ground black pepper to taste
6 oz. shredded mozzarella cheese

Pour oil into a large, heavy skillet over medium heat. Add onion and cook, stirring, until transparent. Stir in garlic and cook until fragrant. Add zucchini; cover and cook about 3 minutes until crisp-tender. Tilt skillet and spoon off all possible oil. Stir in tomato paste and water. Add oregano, basil, salt and pepper. Cook, stirring, until liquid thickens. Set aside at room temperature until ready to use. Reheat and spoon over stove-top pizza, as directed. Sprinkle with cheese and continue to cook pizza, as directed.

Makes sufficient topping and cheese for six 6" to 7" stove-top pizzas.

BRIE AND TOMATO TOPPING

Creamy rich Brie contrasts with intensely flavored black olives and fresh tomatoes, making this easy-to-prepare topping a prize-winner.

4 large, ripe tomatoes
3 to 4 oz. Brie, cut into cubes
1 tablespoon chopped, fresh basil leaves or 1/4 teaspoon dried basil
8 to 10 Italian or Niçoise olives, pitted, cut into slivers

Salt to taste
Coarsely ground black pepper to taste
2 tablespoons freshly grated Romano cheese

Plunge each tomato into a large pan of rapidly boiling water. Hold under cold running water and slip off skins. Hold each tomato over a bowl and cut into thick chunks, letting the chunks drop into bowl. Add Brie, basil, olives, salt and pepper. Set aside at room temperature until ready to use. Drain off liquid. Spoon over stove-top pizza, as directed. Sprinkle with grated cheese and continue to cook, as directed.

Makes sufficient topping and cheese for one 6" to 7" stove-top pizza.

TOMATO-ANCHOVY TOPPING

This topping requires no cooking but should be made only during the summer, when tomatoes are garden-fresh.

2 large, firm-but-ripe tomatoes
2 tablespoons minced fresh
   basil leaves or ½ teaspoon
   dried basil
¼ teaspoon oregano
Sprinkling of hot pepper flakes

1 2-oz. flat tin rolled and caper-
   stuffed anchovy filets,
   drained
2 tablespoons grated Parmesan
   cheese

Plunge each tomato into a large pan of rapidly boiling water. Hold under cold running water and slip off skins. Hold each tomato over a bowl and cut into thick chunks, letting them drop into bowl. Drain off juice and reserve for other use. Sprinkle with basil, oregano and a few hot pepper flakes. Drain and add anchovies. Stir to blend, then set aside until ready to use. Spoon over pizza as directed in stove-top pizza recipe. Sprinkle with cheese. Cover and continue to cook, as directed.

Makes sufficient topping and cheese for six 6" to 7" stove-top pizzas.

AMIGO TOPPING

1 large, ripe tomato
¾ lb. ground beef
1 large onion, peeled, chopped
2 to 3 teaspoons chili powder, or to taste
3 tablespoons tomato sauce or tomato ketchup (preferably the kind labeled "hot")

8 to 10 pimiento-stuffed green olives, sliced
Salt to taste
Coarsely ground black pepper to taste
1 cup shredded sharp cheddar cheese

Cut tomato in half. Gently squeeze out seeds and juice from each half. Place on work surface and cut into thin slivers; blot dry. Set aside.

In a large, heavy skillet over medium heat cook beef, stirring to break up pieces, until no longer pink. Stir in onion and cook until tender. Tilt skillet and spoon off rendered fat. Stir in chili powder and tomato sauce. Add slivered tomato and olives. Season with salt and pepper. Set aside at room temperature until ready to use. Reheat and spoon over stovetop pizza, as directed. Sprinkle with cheese and continue to cook pizza, as directed.

Makes sufficient topping and cheese for six 6" to 7" stovetop pizzas.

6

Appetizer
Pizzas

Call them appetizers, hors d'oeuvres, or just finger-food: a big, beautiful Riviera-style pizza, an elegant French *pissaladière*, or any of the other great-tasting pizzas you'll find in this section are guaranteed to please. Honestly—and we say this only after long experience—nothing else can satisfy so many people so thoroughly for such a small output of effort, money and time.

It's such a relief to know that pizza can be prepared ahead and frozen, ready to reheat just before serving. When it's served hot-from-the-oven, everyone will be impressed by its heady fragrance, its generous size, and its rich, delicious taste. Both you and your guests will love it.

No matter how simple or elegant your party, pizza is never out of place. It's great with beer for a casual gathering, and it's a superb addition to a bountiful buffet table.

It's hard to know which of these pizzas to suggest you try first. Each one has its own special appeal. You might serve the *pissaladière* to people who are especially fond of hearty red wine; the guacamole adaptation for aficionados of pale, golden ale; or the Riviera-style pizza when you are not quite sure what drinks your friends will select. No matter, though: any one of these pizzas will go nicely with whatever beverage you serve.

We have only one suggestion for this appetizing subject. For easy eating, cut your prepared pizza before you serve it. Do not, however, separate the pieces: for dramatic effect, present it so that it appears uncut.

If you prepare your pizza several hours or days ahead of time, cool it in the pan (or on the baking sheet) to room temperature. With a serrated knife, cut it across into strips ½ inch long, then cut the strips diagonally into bite-size, diamond shapes. Next, cover it completely with a wide strip of heavy-duty aluminum foil, in length a little more than double the circumference of your pizza. Holding the foil firmly in place on each side, invert the pizza and remove the pan. Fold short sides of foil inward, bring long sides up and fold, drugstore fashion, to seal and enclose the pizza in a neat package. Store in refrigerator or freezer. When ready to reheat, tear open and pull back foil from bottom of pizza and invert it back into its original pan or onto a large heat-proof platter. Remove top of foil. Reheat just before serving.

Have a great time!

● PISSALADIÈRE

(*Classic Riviera-Style Pizza*)

The French answer to Italian-style pizza. No tomatoes here; just a superbly flavored crust topped with mild, sweet onions, purply-black olives from Nice and piquant anchovy filets. Elegant and positively addictive.

½ cup olive oil
2 lb. yellow or white onions, peeled, chopped
½ teaspoon salt
1 tablespoon chopped fresh rosemary or ½ teaspoon dried rosemary
1 tablespoon fresh basil or ½ teaspoon dried basil
Sprinkling of thyme

2 packages dry yeast
¼ cup lukewarm water (105° F to 110° F)
½ teaspoon sugar
2 to 3 cups all-purpose flour
½ teaspoon additional salt
2 eggs, lightly beaten
½ cup shredded Gruyère cheese
8 to 12 Niçoise olives, cut from stones into slivers

Pour oil into a large heavy skillet over medium heat. Add onions, and cook, stiring frequently, until transparent. Sprinkle with salt. Reduce heat to very low and continue to cook, stirring frequently, about 15 to 20 minutes until onions are deep golden in color.

Remove skillet from heat and drain onions into a colander that has been placed over a bowl. Transfer onions to another bowl and stir in rosemary, basil and thyme. Set aside. Reserve bowl of cooking oil for dough.

Place yeast and sugar in a small bowl; add lukewarm water. Stir once and let stand until yeast has dissolved and mixture is bubbly.

Measure one cup of flour into large mixing bowl and add remaining salt. Stir in yeast mixture; add oil from onions. Mix thoroughly; dough will be sticky. Add lightly beaten eggs and one more cup of flour. Mix until blended. Cover bowl with a clean towel and let rise in a warm, draft-free place about 1 hour until volume doubles.

Preheat oven to 425° F.

Turn dough out onto a lightly floured surface and knead until smooth and elastic, adding as much of the remaining flour as necessary to keep dough from sticking to board.

Pat dough out with the palms of your hands to flatten into an 8″ or 10″ circle. Place circle in a 12″ or 14″ pizza pan and press out evenly to cover bottom and sides of pan. Or, place on a baker's peel, flatten to about ¼″ thickness, then pinch ends up to form a thick edge. Set dough aside for about 30 minutes.

If baking *pissaladière* on a baking stone, place stone on center rack in oven and preheat oven to 450° F. If baking in pizza pan, place rack on lowest position in oven and preheat oven to 425° F.

When oven is fully heated, spoon onions over surface of pizza dough, spreading evenly. Sprinkle with cheese and olives. Slide *pissaladière* from peel onto heated baking stone and reduce oven temperature to 425° F or place *pissaladière* in pan in preheated oven. Bake about 20 minutes until crust is lightly browned.

Makes one 12″ to 14″ *pissaladière*.

● RIVIERA-STYLE PIZZA DOUGH

⅓ cup warm water (105° to 110° F)

1 package dry yeast

¼ teaspoon sugar

2½ cups all-purpose flour

½ teaspoon salt

1 tablespoon sugar

4 tablespoons very cold, firm butter

1 egg

1 egg yolk

Hand Method: Place warm water in a small bowl; sprinkle with ¼ teaspoon sugar and yeast. Let stand until yeast has dissolved and mixture is bubbly. Place flour, salt and 1 tablespoon sugar in a large mixing bowl. Cut butter into small cubes and add to flour mixture. Work with your fingers, two knives or a pastry blender until mixture resembles coarse oatmeal. In another bowl, beat egg and egg yolk until blended; add yeast mixture and blend well. Stir into flour mixture. Turn out on a lightly floured surface and spinkle top of dough lightly with additional flour. Knead until smooth and elastic, adding more flour if needed to keep dough from sticking to surface. Form into a smooth ball.

Processor Method: Pour warm water into a 1-cup measure. Sprinkle with yeast and the ¼ teaspoon sugar. Let stand until yeast has dissolved and mixture is bubbly. Place flour, salt and 1 tablespoon sugar in work bowl of food processor; cover; turn motor off and on several times to mix well. Remove processor cover and, holding butter over bowl, cut into thin slices, letting slices fall into flour. Cover and turn motor on and off several times until butter is mixed into flour and is no longer discernible. In small bowl, beat egg and egg yolk until blended. Stir in yeast mixture. Pour mixture through feed tube of processor; process for about 45 seconds or until dough leaves sides of processor; turn out on a lightly floured surface. Knead several seconds and shape into a ball.

Place ball of dough in a lightly floured bowl; turn dough to flour evenly. Cover bowl with plastic wrap and let stand in a warm, draft-free place about 1½ hours until dough is double in volume.

Turn dough out onto a lightly floured surface and flatten evenly with your hands. Using a rolling pin, roll dough out into a 12″ or 14″ circle. Fold into quarters, center the point in a 12″ or 14″ pizza pan, unfold dough to cover pan. With floured fingers press dough up to cover the sides of pan. Fill, top and bake as directed in individual receipes.

RIVIERA-STYLE PIZZA

Riviera-Style Pizza Dough or
   All-Purpose Pizza Dough (see
   Chapter 3)
Riviera-Style Pizza Sauce (see
   recipe that follows)
$\frac{1}{2}$ cup grated Gruyère cheese
3 thin slices Gruyère cheese,
   each cut diagonally into two
   triangles

12 caper-stuffed rolled anchovy
   filets
12 Basque black olives, pitted,
   cut in half

Prepare pizza dough. Set aside to rise. Prepare sauce and toppings while dough rises.

Adjust oven racks to the lowest and highest positions.

Preheat oven to 425° F. Roll out and arrange pizza dough in a 12″ or 14″ pizza pan. Sprinkle evenly with grated Gruyère. Place on lowest rack of fully preheated oven; bake about 6 minutes or until crust is just faintly golden. Remove from oven. Increase oven temperature to 450° F. When oven is heated, spread crust evenly with sauce. Arrange cheese slices in an attractive design over sauce. Place rolled anchovy filets and black olives between cheese slices. Place pizza on highest rack in oven. Bake for about 10 minutes or until sauce is bubbly hot.

Makes one 12″ to 14″ round pizza.

RIVIERA-STYLE PIZZA SAUCE

2 tablespoons olive oil
2 cloves garlic, minced
1 1-lb. can tomato sauce
$\frac{1}{2}$ cup water
1 tablespoon chopped fresh
   basil or 1 teaspoon dried
   basil
$\frac{1}{2}$ teaspoon dried rosemary

$\frac{1}{4}$ teaspoon thyme
$\frac{1}{2}$ teaspoon sugar
2 bay leaves
1 tablespoon red wine vinegar
$\frac{1}{2}$ teaspoon coarsely ground
   black pepper
Salt to taste

107

Pour oil into large, heavy skillet over low heat. Add garlic and sauté until soft and fragrant. Add tomato sauce, water, herbs, sugar and bay leaves; stir to blend. Simmer over low heat, stirring often, about 20 minutes. Remove bay leaves. Stir in vinegar. Add pepper. Season to taste with salt. Set aside at room temperature until ready to use or refrigerate until needed, but bring to room temperature before using.

Makes 1½ to 2 cups sauce.

RIVIERA-STYLE PIZZA WITH MUSHROOMS AND GARLIC BUTTER

Riviera-Style Pizza Dough or
  All-Purpose Pizza Dough for
  one 12″ to 14″ round pizza
  (see Chapter 3)
4 tablespoons butter
¾ lb. mushrooms, trimmed,
  thinly sliced
4 tablespoons minced shallots
  or green onions
3 cloves garlic, peeled, finely
  minced
1 cup homemade tomato sauce,
  or 1 8-oz. can tomato sauce

4 oz. shredded fontina cheese
1 tablespoon finely minced
  parsley
½ teaspoon dried basil
¼ teaspoon dried oregano
⅛ teaspoon dried rosemary
⅛ teaspoon dried marjoram
¼ cup grated Parmesan cheese
2 tablespoons coarsely shredded mozzarella cheese
2 tablespoons minced chives or
  green onions

Prepare pizza dough. Set aside to rise. While dough rises, prepare filling and topping.

Melt butter in a large, heavy skillet over medium heat. When bubbly, add mushrooms and shallots; cook, stirring, 2 to 3 minutes. Stir in garlic and continue to cook, stirring occasionally, until vegetables are crisp-tender. Remove from heat and set aside until ready to use.

Position rack in center of oven and preheat to 425° F.

When dough has risen, turn out on a lightly floured surface. Shape and place in pizza pan as directed.

Cover bottom of dough evenly with tomato sauce. Sprinkle with fontina cheese, parsley, basil, oregano, rosemary, marjoram and Parmesan cheese. Cover evenly with mushroom mixture. Top with mozzarella and chives. Place in preheated oven and bake 15 to 20 minutes or until crust is lightly browned. Let pizza stand at room temperature about 5 minutes before cutting. Serve hot.

Makes one 12" to 14" round pizza.

PISSALADIÈRE ANOTHER WAY

(*Oblong* Pissaladière *with Creamy Onion Topping*)
The pleasures of Provence are expressed eloquently in yet another version of pizza from the south of France.

Riviera-Style Pizza Dough or
   All-Purpose Pizza Dough for
   oblong pizza (see Chapter 3)
6 thick slices bacon
2 lb. onions, peeled, chopped
1 teaspoon dillweed or caraway
   seeds (optional)
1 teaspoon salt

½ teaspoon pepper
2 tablespoons flour
1 egg
1 egg yolk
½ cup sour cream

Prepare dough. Set aside to rise. While dough rises, prepare topping.

Place bacon in a large, heavy skillet over low heat until fat is rendered and bacon is crisp. Transfer bacon to paper toweling to drain; crumble and set aside. Pour all but about 2 tablespoons of the rendered bacon fat from the skillet (discard the poured-off fat or pour it into a small bowl, cover and refrigerate for another use). Add onions to remaining fat in skillet. Cook and stir over low heat until onions are very soft and pale golden in color. Stir in dillweed or caraway seeds, if desired. Season with salt and pepper. Sprinkle surface evenly with flour and stir until blended.

In a separate bowl beat egg and egg yolk until blended, then stir in sour cream. Add to skillet and stir until mixture thickens. Remove from heat. Set aside at room temperature, or cover and refrigerate until ready to use but bring to room temperature before using.

Preheat oven to 425° F.

When dough has risen, punch down and turn out on a lightly floured surface; pat out into a rectangle about 8" x 12". Place in a 10" x 15" jelly roll pan, and with floured hands press it out to cover bottom and sides of pan evenly. Cover dough on bottom with prepared onion mixture. Sprinkle with crumbled bacon. Bake in preheated oven 15 to 20 minutes until crust is golden brown.

Makes one 10" x 15" oblong pizza.

CRISPY BLUE-CHEESE APPETIZER PIZZA

Mild but distinctive blue cheese is used instead of the traditional mozzarella for this passionately flavorful appetizer. Delizioso!

Riviera-Style Pizza Dough or All-Purpose Pizza Dough for one 12" to 14" round pizza (see Chapter 3)
2 tablespoons olive oil
½ cup finely chopped shallots
1 1-lb. can Italian plum tomatoes and their juice

3 tablespoons tomato paste
1 tablespoon finely chopped fresh basil or 1 teaspoon dried basil
1 teaspoon sugar
½ teaspoon salt
Black pepper to taste
4 oz. crumbled blue cheese

Prepare dough. Set aside to rise. While dough rises prepare sauce and topping.

Pour the oil into a large, heavy skillet over low heat. When hot, add shallots and cook, stirring, until softened. Add tomatoes and their juice. Cook, breaking up the tomatoes into small pieces with tip of a spoon or a spatula. When liquid comes to a boil stir in tomato paste, reduce heat, add basil, sugar, salt and black pepper to taste. Reduce heat to very low and let sauce simmer, stirring occasionally until thickened. Cool to room temperature before using.

Place blue cheese in a small bowl and break apart into very small pieces with the tines of a fork. Refrigerate until ready to use. (If cheese is left at room temperature, the pieces will begin to soften and stick together.)

Preheat oven to 425° F.

When dough has risen, punch down and turn out on a lightly floured surface. Flatten into a flat disk. Turn disk over and sprinkle lightly with flour. With your hands press out into an oval, not round, shape. Turn the dough over and sprinkle lightly with flour. Continue to press, then pull the edges of the dough out until it is about ½" thick. Place oval on a flat baking sheet. Press and pull until dough is no more than ¼" thick. Turn the edges inward and press up to form a thick rim. Spread tomato sauce evenly over surface and sprinkle cheese evenly on top. Bake in preheated oven until edges of dough are lightly browned, sauce is bubbly and cheese is melted.

Let stand at room temperature at least 5 minutes before cutting.

Makes one 10" x 14" oval pizza.

● GUACAMOLE PIZZA

Crisp Pizza Pastry dough (see recipe that follows)
1 small bunch parsley, washed, blotted dry, tough stems removed (enough for ½ cup minced parsley)
1 small bunch green onions
2 medium tomatoes
2 medium avocados (about 1 lb.)
¼ cup lemon or lime juice
1 tablespoon finely minced or grated onion
2 tablespoons chili sauce
¼ teaspoon cumin seed (optional)
Salt to taste
Coarsely ground black pepper to taste
2 or 3 dashes hot pepper sauce (optional)
1 cup sour cream
3 to 4 oz. Monterey Jack cheese, shredded

Prepare pizza dough; shape and bake as directed.

Finely mince parsley; place in a small bowl. Trim and cut stems from onions. Finely chop white bulbs, cut tops across into thin rounds. Place white and green parts in separate bowls. Cut tomatoes in half; gently squeeze out seeds, pulp and juice

111

from each half. Cut halves into narrow strips and blot dry.

Cut avocados in half lengthwise, remove pits and scoop meat into medium-size bowl (reserving 1 pit). Mash avocado pulp with lemon or lime juice until very smooth. Stir in grated onion, chili sauce and, if desired, cumin seed. Season to taste with salt and pepper; if you want an even hotter mixture, add hot pepper sauce. Place one of the avocado pits in the bowl, cover bowl with plastic wrap and refrigerate until ready to use, but no more than 1 hour.

Assemble pizza as close to serving time as possible. Remove and discard pit from avocado mixture. Spoon mixture evenly over baked pizza crust. Spread a thin layer of sour cream evenly over top, covering mixture completely.

Sprinkle minced parsley in a circle over center of tart. Circle parsley with a ring of minced white onion. Then make a ring with tomato strips; surround with a ring of green onion slices. Sprinkle shredded cheese in a ring near the outside crust. If desired, refrigerate pizza until ready to serve, but no more than ½ hour.

Makes one 12" round pizza.

CRISP PIZZA PASTRY

1¾ cups sifted all-purpose flour
4 tablespoons chilled lard or
   vegetable shortening
4 tablespoons chilled butter

1 egg yolk, lightly beaten with 3
   tablespoons ice water
¼ teaspoon salt

Put flour in a mixing bowl; cut chilled lard or vegetable shortening and butter into small cubes. Add to flour and work quickly together with fingertips until mixture forms small, flaky granules, rather like coarse oatmeal. Pour in egg yolk mixture and with a fork, stir to a soft dough.

With your hands, gather dough into a ball, adding any crumbs from the side of the bowl. The dough should feel moist, but not sticky. Place on a lightly floured surface. Roll out into a circle about 13" in diameter. Fold dough in half; lift and lay the fold across the center of a 12" pizza pan and unfold it.

With your fingers, form a rim about ⅓″ high. If desired, re-frigerate the formed dough on the pan for about 30 minutes or until ready to bake.

Preheat oven to 425° F.

With a fork, prick bottom of pastry at about ½″ intervals over entire surface. Bake in preheated oven 15 to 20 minutes or until crust is golden brown. Cool to room temperature be-fore filling, slide pastry onto a large, flat platter or plate. Fill with guacamole mixture, sour cream and topping, no more than 30 minutes before serving.

Makes one 12″ pizza.

● PAMPERED-HOSTESS PIZZAS

These super quick, super delicious pizzas will leave your guests thinking you have an Italian chef in your kitchen.

APPETIZER PIZZAS WITH TOMATO PESTO SAUCE AND FRESH MUSHROOMS

¼ cup olive oil

2 cloves garlic, peeled, crushed

16 frozen, commercial bread dough rolls

2 cups homemade tomato sauce, or 1 1-lb. jar Italian cooking sauce

3 tablespoons Pesto or Parsley Pesto (see Chapter 4) or com-mercial pesto alla Genovese (basil sauce)

¼ lb. mushrooms, trimmed, thinly sliced

½ cup grated Parmesan cheese

6 oz. shredded mozzarella cheese

1 whole pimiento, cut into thin slivers

Pour oil into a small skillet. Add garlic. Place over very low heat until garlic is deep golden (do not allow to brown). With slotted spoon remove and discard garlic; bring oil to room temperature.

Dip each frozen roll in the garlic-seasoned oil and turn to coat on all sides. Arrange rolls, so they are not touching each other, on a long, flat baking sheet. Set aside at room temperature about 1 hour until volume doubles.

One at a time, place each roll on a floured work surface, and with floured hands flatten out into a circle about 4" in diameter. Roll edges inward and up to form small pizzas. Place, not touching each other, on a clean baking sheet.

Preheat oven to 425° F.

Combine tomato and pesto sauce; blend well. Spoon about 1 tablespoon of mixture over each small pizza, spread out evenly. Top with sliced mushrooms, dividing evenly. Sprinkle with cheeses and pimiento slivers.

Bake in preheated oven until crust is lightly browned.

Serve hot or bring to room temperature and reheat just before serving.

If desired, pizzas may be made ahead and frozen. Place in single layer on flat surface in freezer until firm. Wrap airtight and store in freezer up to 1 month. Reheat frozen pizzas in 350° F oven.

Makes 16 small pizzas.

ARTICHOKE-HEART PIZZAS

There is no limit to the number of different ways you can top these easy, quick-to-make pizzas, but here's one that's a must.

1 6-oz. jar imported marinated artichoke hearts, quartered
12 frozen, commercial bread dough rolls
1 cup homemade tomato sauce or 1 8-oz. can tomato sauce

Basil to taste
Oregano to taste
¼ lb. fontina cheese, cut into small cubes
¼ cup grated Parmesan cheese

Drain marinade from artichoke hearts into a small bowl. Set artichoke hearts aside. One at a time, dip each frozen roll in marinade, turning to coat all sides. Arrange rolls so they are not touching each other, on a long, flat baking sheet. Set aside at room temperature about 1 hour until volume doubles.

Coarsely chop artichoke quarters.

When rolls have risen, place one at a time on a floured work surface. With floured hands, flatten each one into a 4" circle. Turn edges inward and up to form miniature pizzas.

Preheat oven to 425° F.

Spoon about 1 tablespoon of tomato sauce onto each pizza round. Sprinkle with basil and oregano. Top with chopped artichoke hearts, dividing evenly. Sprinkle each with cheeses.

Bake in preheated oven until crust is lightly browned.

Serve hot, or cool to room temperature then reheat just before serving. Or place in single layer on flat surface in freezer until firm. Wrap airtight and store in freezer up to 1 month.

Reheat frozen pizzas in 350° F oven.

Makes 12 pizzas.

FRESH-TOMATO PIZZAS

Summertime, and pizza making is easier and more delicious than ever.

¼ cup olive oil

12 frozen, commercial bread dough rolls

3 tablespoons grated Parmesan cheese

12 thick slices sun-ripened tomatoes

Salt

1 cup shredded mozzarella cheese

1 2-oz. flat tin anchovy filets, drained

Pour olive oil into a small bowl. Dip each frozen roll in oil, turning to coat evenly. Arrange rolls, so they are not touching each other, on a long, flat baking sheet. Set aside in warm, draft-free place until volume doubles.

When rolls have risen, place one at a time on a floured work surface, and with floured hands flatten each one to a 4"

circle. Roll edges inward and up to form rims, making small pizzas. Sprinkle each evenly with grated Parmesan cheese.
Preheat oven to 425° F.

Place pizzas in preheated oven and bake for about 10 minutes. Set aside.

Sprinkle each tomato slice lightly, but evenly, with salt. Place on triple thickness of paper toweling and let drain for about 15 minutes.

Place one tomato slice on each pizza; sprinkle evenly with mozzarella cheese; crisscross 2 anchovy filets on top.

Return pizzas to preheated oven and bake until cheese has melted and crust is lightly browned.

Serve hot.

Makes 12 pizzas.

● PIZZA POR AMORE

Whole artichoke hearts are the foundations for these elegant pizzas. Expensive, but worth it for someone you love. Four are adequate as the first course of a romantic, "just the two of us" meal.

One small tomato
4 whole artichoke hearts, canned or fresh (see instructions that follow)
4 teaspoons Pesto or Parsley Pesto (see Chapter 4) or canned, imported pesto alla Genovese

8 teaspoons grated Parmesan cheese
1 thin slice mozzarella cheese, cut into ½" x ¼" strips
4 Italian or Niçoise olives, cut from stone into slivers

Cut tomato in half, gently squeeze seeds and juice from each half; cut into thin strips, blot dry; set aside. Prepare fresh artichoke hearts as directed below, or drain canned artichoke hearts. Spoon a teaspoon of pesto sauce into each. Sprinkle each with about 1 teaspoon of grated Parmesan cheese, dividing evenly. Cover with strips of mozzarella and olive slivers.
Preheat oven to 400° F.

Place pizzas on a flat baking sheet; bake until cheeses have melted.

Serve warm or at room temperature.

Makes 4 small artichoke pizzas.

PREPARING FRESH ARTICHOKE HEARTS

Fill a large, stainless steel or enamelized cast iron pot with water, and bring to a boil over high heat. Add 2 tablespoons salt and ¼ cup vinegar or fresh lemon juice. Cut stems from artichokes and discard. Add artichokes to boiling water. Boil 35 to 40 minutes or until the leaves can be easily pulled off and the bottoms are tender. Remove with slotted spoon from boiling water and turn upside down to drain. When cool, pull off all the leaves. (But don't throw the leaves away. Put them in a bowl, cover with a mild vinaigrette dressing and refrigerate to use the next night or even two or three days later as an appetizer with a piquant dip.) Using a sturdy spoon, carefully scrape and pull all of the fuzzy, prickly bottom portion, the choke, from the hearts. Trim the bottoms so they will sit upright, without wobbling. Use immediately or rub all surfaces of each with lemon juice and refrigerate until ready to use.

● KOHLRABI PIZZA

Your weight-conscious friends will love you for this flavorful low-calorie pizza appetizer.

1 large kohlrabi (about 4″ in diameter)
Salt
Water
Oil
4 teaspoons thick pizza or tomato sauce
2 thin slices prosciutto or imported Italian soppressata

4 imported Italian sun-dried tomatoes, each pulled in half
4 teaspoons grated Parmesan cheese
2 thin slices whole-milk mozzarella cheese, cut into slivers

117

Peel kohlrabi, cut off ends and reserve for other use. Cut center of kohlrabi into 4 thick slices. Place slices in single layer in a large skillet, sprinkle with salt, add water to cover. Bring to boil; let boil 1 minute. Drain immediately into a colander and rinse under cold running water. Blot dry.

Preheat oven to 425° F.

Rub each kohlrabi slice with oil on both sides. Place on a flat baking sheet. Spread each with pizza or tomato sauce. Cover each with remaining ingredients, in order listed, dividing evenly.

Bake in preheated oven until cheeses have melted.

Cut into wedges and serve warm as hors d'oeuvres. Or place each pizza on a small appetizer plate and serve as a first course. Provide small knives and forks for easy eating.

Serves 8 as hors d'oeuvres, 4 as a first course.

● MUSHROOM PIZZAS LORIANA

Select firm, white, giant-size mushrooms with caps that are closed or only slightly opened around the stems for these hot pizza hors d'oeuvres from Italy.

12 large mushrooms

2 tablespoons butter

2 tablespoons minced green onion

1 tablespoon minced green pepper

1 clove garlic, peeled, minced (optional)

1 egg

3 tablespoons ricotta cheese

2 tablespoons commerical Italian-seasoned bread crumbs

2 tablespoons finely chopped pimiento-stuffed olives

Pinch of oregano

Salt and pepper to taste

1 tablespoon grated Parmesan cheese

Preheat oven to 375° F.

Wipe each mushroom clean with damp paper towel. Gently twist stems from each, leaving cavity for filling. Trim ends from stems, chop coarsely.

Melt butter in a large, heavy skillet over medium heat until foamy. When foaming begins to subside, place mushroom caps in single layer in skillet, cap side down. Cook until liquid forms in cavity; turn and cook other side for about 1 minute; remove with slotted spoon and arrange cavity side up in a long, shallow baking dish.

In same skillet, add onions, green pepper, garlic and chopped mushroom stems. Cook and stir until onions are tender, about 5 minutes. Remove mixture from skillet and set aside to cool.

In a large bowl, beat egg and ricotta cheese until blended. Stir in onion mixture, bread crumbs and olives. Season with oregano, salt and pepper. With a small spoon, fill each mushroom cap with mixture. Sprinkle each evenly with grated Parmesan cheese. Bake in preheated oven 15 to 20 minutes or until tops are lightly browned.

Serve hot.

Makes 12 two-bite-size mushroom pizza appetizers.

7

Double-Quick Pizzas

You've been extra busy, and you've worked late every night this week, so of course you don't have the time or inclination to prepare what you need and want: something extra-flavorful and satisfying, like a great big, beautiful, homemade pizza. Fortunately, being busy, overworked, and too tired to cook doesn't mean you have to settle for second best.

No need to dash out through the homebound crowd and buck the late shoppers' crush at your supermarket to buy a frozen pizza with a skimpy topping, or rush to the take-out shop for an over-priced, under-seasoned one. You can prepare a double-quick pizza with grand Italian taste at home in the relative quiet of your own kitchen.

With a little planning, you can always have basic pizza-making ingredients on hand. No time to make pizza dough from scratch? Use a flavorful Italian-style loaf, crusty pita pocket bread or English muffins instead. Hopefully, you will have a cup or so of homemade pizza sauce in your freezer. If not, don't despair. Use that can of pizza sauce you have on your kitchen shelf. As with all canned sauces produced for so-called "mass market" appeal it will undoubtedly be too mild for your taste. But that can be remedied easily. Just dump the contents of the can into a saucepan placed over low heat and "up" the flavor to your taste by adding a bit of dried oregano and—if you have it, lucky you—some chopped, fresh basil from your windowsill herb garden. Now stir, heat and taste. If you find it a bit sweet, stir in a few teaspoons of red wine vinegar plus a dash of coarsely ground black pepper; that should do the trick. As for cheeses, use what you have on hand. Almost any good melting cheese tastes grand on a pizza. If what you have is a little dry or old after too long a stay in your refrigerator, that can be remedied, too. Grate or chop it into small pieces, place it in a bowl and add a tablespoon or so of good quality olive oil. Stir and let stand about 15 minutes, or a bit longer, while you set the table or watch the news on TV.

What else? Well, look through this chapter and you'll find

quite a few ideas. Among them: double-quick pizza crusts made with either all-purpose flour or pie crust mix, plus a little dry yeast to give authentic pizza flavor; a baker's dozen or so of quickly put together toppings; and more. All prove that you don't need much time or money for a super delicious quick-to-the-table pizza meal.

● AFTER-WORK, HURRY-UP PIZZA

1 tablespoon olive or vegetable oil
1 small onion, peeled, chopped
1 small clove garlic, peeled, minced
1 8-oz. can tomato sauce
1 4-oz. can sautéed-in-butter mushrooms
½ teaspoon dried basil
¼ teaspoon dried oregano
¼ teaspoon coarsely ground black pepper

Salt to taste
½ cup warm water (105° F to 110° F)
⅛ teaspoon sugar
1 package dry yeast
1 cup plus 2 tablespoons flour
¼ teaspoon salt
6 oz. shredded mozzarella cheese
3¼ oz. sliced pepperoni
½ cup grated Parmesan or Romano cheese

Pour oil into large, heavy skillet over medium heat. Add onion, cook and stir about 5 minutes, add garlic and continue to cook until vegetables are tender. Pour in tomato sauce. Drain and add mushrooms. Season with basil, oregano and pepper. Cook, stirring occasionally, until sauce is bubbly hot. Taste and add salt if desired. Remove from heat and let cool while preparing pizza dough.

Preheat oven to 425° F. Lightly grease a 12″ pizza pan.

Pour warm water into a large mixing bowl. Add sugar. Sprinkle surface with yeast. Let stand for about 5 minutes or until bubbly. Stir in flour and salt. Dough will be soft and sticky; use a spoon dipped in flour to spread it evenly in greased pan. Bake in preheated oven for 5 minutes. Remove from oven and spread with tomato sauce mixture. Sprinkle with half of mozzarella. Arrange pepperoni slices, slightly overlapping, over cheese. Sprinkle with remaining mozzarella and top evenly with grated Parmesan or Romano cheese. Return pizza to heated oven and bake 10 to 15 minutes or until crust is lightly browned.

Makes one 12″ round pizza.

● EASY PARMESAN PIZZA CRUST

2½ cups all-purpose flour
¼ cup freshly grated Parmesan
  cheese
2¼ teaspoons baking powder

1 teaspoon salt
¼ cup vegetable shortening
¼ cup butter
¾ cup milk

Preheat oven to 425°F.

Butter two 12″ to 14″ pizza pans. Set aside.

In a large bowl, combine flour, cheese, baking powder and salt; blend well. With your hands, work vegetable shortening and butter into flour mixture until mixture resembles coarse oatmeal. Gradually stir in milk; stir until mixture leaves sides of bowl and can be formed into a soft ball. Knead for about 1 minute while still in bowl. Turn out on a lightly floured surface. Divide dough in half. Roll each half into a 13″ to 15″ circle. Transfer each circle to a pizza pan. With your fingers, press edges of dough up sides of pans to form slight rims. Bake in preheated oven for 10 minutes; cool on rack.

Makes two 12″ to 14″ pizza crusts.

Note: This pizza crust can be made ahead and left at room temperature for several hours, or refrigerated for up to two days.

EASY PARMESAN PIZZA CRUST WITH PESTO FILLING
This delicious, simple-to-make pizza features crisp crust and mellow rich filling with basil.

Easy Parmesan Pizza Crust
1 1-lb. can Italian-style
  tomatoes
1 lb. shredded mozzarella
  cheese
¼ cup grated Parmesan cheese
½ cup pine nuts, crushed
1 tablespoon minced fresh basil
  leaves or 1 teaspoon dried
  crumbled basil leaves

½ teaspoon salt
¼ teaspoon pepper
2 teaspoons olive oil
½ lb. fresh mushrooms,
  trimmed, sliced

Prepare and prebake 2 pizza crusts.

Preheat oven to 425° F.

Drain tomatoes in a colander set over a bowl. (Reserve juice for other use.) Add mozzarella, Parmesan, pine nuts, basil, salt and pepper. Blend well. Stir in sliced mushrooms.

Brush each prebaked crust with 1 teaspoon olive oil. Fill each crust with tomato-cheese mixture, dividing evenly. Bake 15 to 20 minutes in preheated oven until crust is lightly browned.

Makes two 12″ to 14″ round pizzas.

EASY PARMESAN PIZZA CRUST WITH MARGHERITA TOPPINGS
This pizza brings Italy right to your table.

Easy Parmesan Pizza Crust
¼ cup grated Parmesan cheese
2 cups homemade pizza sauce
  or 1 1-lb. can pizza sauce

2 cups shredded whole-milk
  mozzarella cheese
1 cup slivered fontina cheese
¼ lb. soppressata

Prepare and prebake 2 pizza crusts.

Preheat oven to 425° F.

Sprinkle each crust evenly with half of the Parmesan cheese; cover each with pizza sauce, dividing evenly. Top each with half of the mozzarella and fontina cheeses and arrange half of the soppressata on top.

Bake in preheated oven until crust is lightly browned.

Makes two 12" to 14" round pizzas.

● POPOVER PIZZA

You might call this a pizza in reverse: the topping is on the bottom and the crust on top. It's a delicious surprise.

1 lb. ground beef

1 large onion, peeled, chopped

2 cups Classic Pizza Sauce (see Chapter 4) or 1 1-lb. can marinara sauce

1 6-oz. can sautéed-in-butter mushrooms

1/4 cup water

8 to 10 pimiento-stuffed green olives

1/4 teaspoon dried oregano

1/4 teaspoon dried basil

1/4 teaspoon salt

8 oz. thinly sliced whole-milk mozzarella cheese

2 eggs

1 cup milk

1 tablespoon vegetable oil

1 cup sifted all-purpose flour

1/2 teaspoon salt

1/2 cup grated Parmesan cheese

Preheat oven to 400° F.

Grease a 9" x 15" x 2" baking pan.

Cook beef in a large, heavy skillet, breaking it up as it cooks until no longer pink. Stir in onion, cook until tender. Add sauce, mushrooms, water, olives, herbs and salt. Simmer

125

about 10 minutes. Spoon into prepared pan; top with slices of cheese. Place in preheated oven.

In a large bowl beat eggs, milk and oil with electric mixer until foamy. Beat in flour and salt until batter is smooth. Spoon batter over hot meat mixture, spreading to cover completely. Sprinkle with grated cheese.

Bake in preheated oven 30 minutes or until puffed and deep golden brown.

Cut into squares; serve while hot and puffy.

Makes 6 servings.

● POTATO-CRUST PIZZA

This recipe evolved from our great passion for pizzas and our all-time love of potatoes.

3 medium potatoes (about 1½ lb.)
1 large onion, peeled, chopped
Salt
2 tablespoons olive or vegetable oil
1 teaspoon additional salt
1½ cups flour
2 large sun-ripened tomatoes
6 oz. shredded mozzarella cheese

6 to 8 thin slices pepperoni or other cooked sausage
3 to 4 oz. shredded fontina cheese
1 tablespoon chopped fresh basil or ½ teaspoon dried basil
1 tablespoon chopped fresh oregano or ½ teaspoon dried oregano

Lightly grease a 12″ round pizza pan. Set aside.

Peel and slice potatoes, letting the slices fall into a large bowl of heavily salted cold water. Drain and place slices in a large saucepan. Add chopped onion. Cover with water by about 2″. Bring to full boil then reduce heat and let simmer until vegetables are very tender. Drain thoroughly. Place in a large mixing bowl and while still hot mash until very smooth (onion will blend and mash like potatoes). Add oil, beating with whisk or fork until blended into potato mixture. Stir in 1 teaspoon salt and the flour and mix to a soft dough. Turn out onto lightly greased pizza pan and press with your hands to cover pan completely. Push edges up to form a slightly thicker rim.

Preheat oven to 400° F.

Trim ends from tomatoes and cut into thick slices; place slices in single layer on a double thickness of paper towels. Sprinkle each slice lightly with salt; let stand for about 10 minutes, drain and blot dry. Arrange slices slightly overlapping in a circle over potato dough. Sprinkle evenly with mozzarella. Arrange pepperoni slices on top of tomatoes. Sprinkle with fontina cheese, basil and oregano. Bake in preheated oven 15 to 20 minutes or until edges are brown and cheese bubbly.

Serve hot.

Serves 4 to 6.

● TEXAS CORNBREAD PIZZA

You might call this Italian-inspired Tex-Mex pizza.

1 lb. ground beef
1 large onion, peeled, chopped
1 cup homemade tomato sauce
    or 1 8-oz. can tomato sauce
½ teaspoon cumin
½ teaspoon oregano
1 teaspoon salt
1 teaspoon chili powder
1 4-oz. can chopped jalapeño
    peppers
1½ cups milk
1 teaspoon vinegar
1½ cups cornmeal
½ cup flour
1 teaspoon additional salt
1 egg
2 teaspoons baking powder
½ teaspoon baking soda
¼ cup mild vegetable oil
1 cup chopped or shredded
    Monterey Jack, mild American or mozzarella cheese

Cook and stir meat in a large, heavy skillet over medium heat until no longer pink. Add onion, cook until tender. Pour in tomato sauce. Season with cumin, oregano, salt and chili powder. Stir in chopped peppers. Bring to boil, stirring. Set aside.

Pour milk into a 2-cup measure; stir in vinegar. Set aside for about 5 minutes.

Preheat oven to 400° F.

In a large bowl, combine cornmeal, flour and salt.

Lightly grease a 10″ or 12″ pizza pan. Place in preheated oven.

Add, without stirring, the milk-vinegar mixture and remaining ingredients to cornmeal mixture, then stir to mix thoroughly. Spoon immediately into heated pizza pan and top with meat mixture.

Bake in preheated oven about 20 minutes. Sprinkle evenly with cheese. Bake a final 10 minutes or until cheese has melted. Serve hot.

Makes 4 to 6 servings.

● BAKING-MIX PIZZA DOUGH

Although this dough doesn't rise, it still has that great yeast taste and aroma.

2 cups commercial all-purpose baking mix

1 teaspoon yeast

6 tablespoons warm water (105° to 110° F)

1 tablespoon olive oil, room temperature

Additional baking mix, as needed

In a large bowl, combine baking mix and yeast; stir to blend. Add warm water and oil. Stir to a soft dough. Turn out on a lightly floured surface, knead about 30 seconds. Form into a ball. Let stand about 20 minutes. Flatten ball with floured hands. Using a rolling pin, start from center and roll dough out into a 12″ circle. Roll loosely over pin. Unroll over a 12″ pizza pan. Gently press dough into pan and up sides. Fill and bake as directed in individual recipes.

Makes one 12″ to 14″ round pizza crust.

PIZZA ROLL

In this country most people think of pizza as a flat, round dough topped with delicious things. But in Italy pizza can be a two-crust pie, or a turnover filled with any savory mixture, or dough with filling, shaped and baked in any number of different ways. This version is rolled into an elegant luncheon dish to be eaten with a knife and fork.

Baking-Mix Pizza Dough
1 lb. Italian-style bulk sausage
  meat
1 onion, peeled, finely chopped
1 1-lb. can Italian-style plum
  tomatoes

4 oz. coarsely shredded
  mozzarella cheese
1 cup homemade pizza or
  tomato sauce or 1 8-oz. can
  pizza or tomato sauce

Prepare pizza dough. Turn out on lightly floured surface, knead several minutes, shape into a ball; set aside.

Place sausage meat in a large, heavy skillet over medium heat. Cook, stirring and breaking up meat with the tip of a wooden spoon or spatula, until well-browned and all fat is rendered. With a slotted spoon, transfer meat to a colander; set aside to drain. Pour off and discard all but about 1 tablespoon of rendered fat from the skillet. Add onion and sauté about 5 minutes until tender.

Pour off liquid from tomatoes (reserve liquid for other use). Add tomatoes to skillet with onions, and chop with the tip of a spatula. Add drained sausage meat; stir to blend ingredients. Set aside.

Preheat oven to 450° F. Roll out dough to a 12" or 13" x 8" rectangle. Spread with sausage mixture. Sprinkle evenly with cheese. Starting at a long end, roll the dough up, jelly roll fashion, and pinch the seams together on the bottom. Place on a long, flat baking sheet, seam side down. Cover lightly with a clean dish towel and let stand for about 20 minutes.

Bake in preheated oven for 20 to 25 minutes.

While roll bakes, heat tomato sauce until bubbly. Keep hot until ready to serve.

Cut baked roll into thick slices and place on serving plates. Top each slice with some of the hot sauce. Serve at once.

Makes 6 servings.

● DOUBLE-EASY BAKING-MIX PIZZA

3 cups biscuit baking mix
1 teaspoon paprika
¾ cup water
1 lb. ground beef
1 1¼-oz. package pizza seasoning mix

1 1-lb. can stewed tomatoes
1 4½-oz. can sliced mushrooms, drained
2 cups shredded mozzarella cheese (about ½ lb.)

Preheat oven to 425° F.

Lightly grease a 15″ x 10″ jelly roll pan or rimmed baking sheet.

In a large bowl, combine baking mix and paprika; stir to blend. Add water and stir until soft dough forms. Turn out on a lightly floured work surface. Gently form dough into a ball. Sprinkle lightly with additional flour. Knead 18 to 20 times. Pat dough out into rectangle about 8″ x 10″. Place on greased baking pan. With floured hands, pat evenly over bottom and sides of pan. Set aside.

In a large, heavy skillet over medium heat, cook beef, stirring to crumble, until browned. Drain off drippings. Stir in seasoning mix. Add tomatoes. Drain and add mushrooms. Cook and stir about 5 minutes. Remove from heat and cool to room temperature. Spoon evenly over pizza dough. Top with grated cheese. Bake in preheated oven about 20 minutes until golden brown.

Makes one 10″ x 15″ oblong pizza.

● UPSIDE-DOWN PIZZA

With great right-side-up flavor.

½ lb. sweet Italian sausage links

1 cup homemade tomato sauce or 1 8-oz. can tomato sauce

½ cup water

1 1½-oz. package pizza sauce mix

2 cups shredded mozzarella cheese

1 cup commercial biscuit baking mix

1 cup milk

2 eggs

With the point of a small, sharp knife prick sausage in several places on both sides. Place in a small saucepan; pour in enough water to come about halfway up sides of links. Place over medium heat; let simmer until all water has evaporated. Cook, turning links occasionally, until lightly browned on all sides. Set aside until cool; cut into thick slices.

In a saucepan, combine tomato sauce, water and pizza sauce mix. Simmer over low heat about 5 minutes. Pour into a square 8″ x 8″ baking dish. Arrange sausage slices on top and cover evenly with cheese.

Preheat oven to 350° F.

In a bowl, combine biscuit mix, milk and eggs; blend well. Pour over mixture in baking dish.

Bake in preheated oven 30 to 35 minutes or until cheese has melted.

Makes 4 to 6 servings.

● PIE-CRUST PIZZA DOUGH

This is the fastest pizza dough you can make, yet it's utterly delicious—crisp, thin and yeasty.

¼ cup warm water (105° to 110° F)

1½ teaspoons yeast

⅛ teaspoon sugar

1 9-oz. package pie dough mix

Flour, as needed

Pour warm water into a large mixing bowl, sprinkle with yeast and sugar. Let stand about 5 minutes until bubbly. Add pie dough mix and stir to a soft dough. Turn out on a lightly floured surface and knead about 4 minutes, adding additional flour if dough seems sticky. Let rest about 10 minutes. With a rolling pin, roll dough out into a 12″ circle. Then, roll it over pin and unroll onto a 12″ pizza pan. With floured hands press dough to cover bottom and sides of pan evenly.

Preheat oven to 425° F.

Cover dough with desired sauce and toppings. Bake in center rack of oven 10 to 15 minutes until crust is lightly browned.

Makes one 12″ round pizza.

PIE-CRUST PIZZA WITH FRESH ZUCCHINI AND TOMATO SAUCE

This remarkable, warm-weather main-course pizza is covered with a sauce of zucchini and fresh ripe tomatoes, then topped with Camembert and mozzarella cheeses.

Pie-Crust Pizza Dough

2 large, ripe tomatoes

2 medium zucchini

3 tablespoons olive oil

1 tablespoon chopped, fresh basil or one teaspoon dried basil

2 cloves garlic, peeled, crushed to a paste

½ teaspoon red wine vinegar

1 teaspoon sugar

1 teaspoon salt

Pepper to taste

2 tablespoons tomato paste

½ cup water

6 oz. Camembert cheese, coarsely chopped

6 oz. coarsely grated mozzarella cheese

Prepare pizza crust. Form into a ball, cover loosely with a clean dish towel and let stand while preparing sauce and toppings.

Plunge tomatoes into a large saucepan of boiling water

for 1 minute. Hold under cold, running water and slip off skins. Cut crosswise in half; squeeze halves to remove seeds. Place in work bowl of food processor or blender; process or blend until puréed. Set aside. Coarsely grate zucchini.

Pour oil into a large, heavy skillet over medium-high heat. When hot, add zucchini, basil and garlic; stir-fry about 30 seconds until zucchini is wilted. Stir in puréed tomatoes, vinegar, sugar, salt and pepper; add tomato paste and water. Cook, stirring, until sauce is thick and bubbly hot. Remove from heat; set aside.

Roll out dough and shape in pizza pan, as directed.

Preheat oven to 425° F. Spread dough evenly with zucchini-tomato sauce. Sprinkle sauce with cheeses. Bake in preheated oven about 15 minutes until crust is lightly browned.

Makes one 12″ round pizza.

PIZZA CUPS

Pie-Crust Pizza Dough
2 cups Italian Meat Sauce for
  Pizza (see Chapter 4), or 1
  1-lb. can Italian cooking
  sauce with meat flavor
1 small green pepper, seeded,
  chopped

3 oz. thinly sliced pepperoni,
  each slice cut into quarters
8 oz. shredded mozzarella
  cheese

Preheat oven to 400° F.

Lightly grease a 12-cup muffin pan with olive or vegetable oil. Set aside. Prepare dough as directed. Roll dough into a rectangle about 1/8″ thick. Use a 4″ round cookie cutter to cut dough into circles. Press circles into prepared muffin pan.

In a bowl, combine sauce, green pepper and pepperoni. Spoon into dough cups. Sprinkle each with cheese, dividing evenly. Bake 15 minutes or until cheese is melted.

Makes 12 pizza cups.

133

● SNACK-TIME TV PIZZAS

2 tablespoons olive or vegetable oil
1 small green pepper, seeded, cut into narrow strips
¾ lb. ground Italian-style bulk sausage or similar bulk sausage

1 6-oz. can tomato sauce
1 tablespoon minced onion
1 teaspoon Italian seasoning
1 10-oz. can refrigerator biscuits (10 biscuits)
½ to ¾ cup shredded mozzarella cheese

Pour oil into a large, heavy skillet over medium heat. When hot, add green pepper and sauté until crisp-tender. Remove with slotted spoon, drain and set aside. Pour used oil from skillet; add sausage. Cook until browned, stirring to crumble. Drain off drippings. Pour in tomato sauce. Add onion and seasoning. Add sautéed green pepper strips. Cook, stirring frequently, about 5 minutes until sauce is bubbly hot. Remove from heat and set aside.

Preheat oven to 400° F.

Remove biscuits from can and, one at a time, place on lightly floured work surface. Using a rolling pin, roll out into circle about ¼" thick. Press with fingers to form rim about ⅓" high. Place on a long, shallow baking sheet. Spoon sausage-sauce mixture into each, dividing evenly. Sprinkle each with cheese. Place in preheated oven and bake for 10 to 12 minutes.

Makes 10 pizzas.

● ITALIAN-BREAD PIZZAS

Use long, fat loaves of Italian-style bread with crisp but not thick crust to make these pizzas easier than pie but just as Italian.

134

ITALIAN-BREAD PIZZAS WITH FOUR CHEESES

4 oz. slivered imported Italian provolone cheese
4 oz. chopped fontina cheese
8 oz. mozzarella cheese
¼ cup grated Parmesan cheese

1 tablespoon olive oil
1 long, fat loaf Italian-style bread (about 1 lb.)
1 cup pimiento-stuffed olives

Combine cheeses in a mixing bowl. Add olive oil; toss to blend. Set aside.

Preheat oven to 350° F.

Cut ends from bread loaf (reserve ends for other use); cut across into 3 equal portions, cut each portion lengthwise in half, scoop out soft centers. Place on a long, flat baking sheet. Spoon cheese mixture equally into each. Top each with sliced olives. Bake in preheated oven until cheeses have melted. Serve hot.

Makes 6 small pizzas.

ITALIAN-BREAD PIZZAS WITH SAUSAGE FILLING

1 lb. bulk pork sausage meat
1 1-lb. can Italian-style plum tomatoes and their juice
1 teaspoon mixed Italian seasonings
1 teaspoon dried oregano
1 long, fat loaf Italian-style bread (about 1 lb.)

Olive oil
½ lb. shredded mozzarella cheese
2 tablespoons grated Parmesan cheese
1 teaspoon dried, crushed red pepper

In a large, heavy skillet over medium heat cook sausage meat until lightly browned. Spoon off all rendered fat. Add tomatoes and their juice. Cook, stirring occasionally, until all liquid has evaporated. Stir in Italian seasonings and oregano. Remove from heat and cool to room temperature.

Cut end pieces from bread loaf (reserve ends for other

use). Cut across into 3 equal portions, slice each portion lengthwise in half, scoop out soft centers. Brush each scooped out half lightly with olive oil. Place on a long, flat baking sheet. Place under high broiler heat only until very lightly browned. Cool to room temperature.

Preheat oven to 350° F. Spoon sausage mixture into each scooped out bread section, dividing evenly. Sprinkle each with cheeses; sprinkle cheese with dried red pepper. Bake in preheated oven until cheeses have melted. Serve hot.

Makes 6 small pizzas.

ITALIAN-BREAD PIZZAS WITH CRISP SAUSAGE SLICES AND FONTINA CHEESE

Spicy sausage and mellow fontina cheese are a perfect combination of flavors for these "sure to please" double-quick pizzas.

1 lb. spicy Italian link sausage	2 tablespoons grated Parmesan
1 cup homemade pizza sauce or	cheese
1 8-oz. can pizza sauce	2 tablespoons minced fresh
1 long, fat loaf Italian-style	basil or 2 teaspoons dried
bread (about 1 lb.)	basil
8 oz. fontina cheese, coarsely	
chopped	

With a small, sharp knife prick sausage links in several places on both sides. Place in a small skillet. Pour in enough water to come about halfway up sides of links. Cook over medium heat until all liquid has evaporated, then continue to cook, turning sausage links frequently, until lightly browned on all sides. Remove from heat, cool to room temperature, then cut across into thin slices. Pour rendered fat from skillet and return sausage slices to it; pour in pizza sauce. Let simmer over low heat for 5 to 10 minutes. Set aside.

Cut ends from bread loaf (reserve ends for other use). Cut across into 3 equal portions, cut each lengthwise in half, scoop out soft centers.

Preheat oven to 350° F.

Place scooped out bread slices on a long, flat baking sheet. Spoon sausage mixture into each, dividing evenly. Sprinkle each with cheeses and basil.

Bake in preheated oven until cheeses have melted. Serve hot.

Makes 6 small pizzas.

● NEAPOLITAN LOAF PIZZA

Serve this loaf hot with the most elaborate antipasto you can devise.

1 long, fat loaf Italian-style
   bread (about 1 lb.)
¼ cup olive oil
¼ teaspoon dried basil leaves,
   crumbled
8 thin slices mozzarella cheese

8 thin slices Genoa salami
8 tomato slices, about ¼" thick
Approximately 2 tablespoons
   grated Parmesan or romano
   cheese

Make 15 cuts in bread loaf, making 16 equal slices, but do not cut all the way through bottom crust. In a small bowl, combine olive oil and basil. Spread on all cut surfaces of bread.

Preheat oven to 350° F.

Place sliced loaf on an ungreased baking sheet. In first cut place 1 slice of mozzarella, 1 slice of salami and 1 slice of tomato. Place nothing in second cut. Place 1 slice cheese, salami and tomato in third cut. Repeat until all ingredients are used.

Bake in preheated oven until bread is hot and cheeses are melted.

To serve, cut through bottom crust at unfilled cuts. Serve hot.

Makes 8 servings.

● OPEN-FACE PIZZA SANDWICH

Mama mia! *You never had pizza so easy, so good.*

1 large, round loaf country-style
   Italian bread
6 thin slices provolone cheese
6 thick slices sun-ripened
   tomatoes
¼ cup grated Parmesan cheese

1 6-oz. package thinly sliced
   pepperoni
6 to 8 large mushrooms,
   trimmed, thinly sliced
1 cup shredded mozzarella
   cheese

With a serrated knife, cut bottom and top from bread loaf, leaving a center slice about 1″ thick. Reserve top and bottom slices for other use.

Preheat oven to 425° F.

Place bread slice on flat baking sheet; cover evenly with provolone cheese slices. Top with tomato slices. Sprinkle with grated Parmesan cheese. Arrange pepperoni slices in a circle on top. Cover with mushroom slices. Sprinkle evenly with mozzarella. Bake in preheated oven until cheeses are melted and pizza is hot right down to the bread.

Serve hot, cut into thick wedges.

Serves four.

● SLOPPY PIZZA

An Italian version of a sloppy Joe.

1 lb. lean beef stew meat, cut
   into ½″ cubes
2 tablespoons olive oil
2 cups homemade pizza sauce
   or 1 1-lb. can pizza sauce

½ cup water
4 small zucchini, trimmed,
   coarsely chopped
1 teaspoon oregano
4 thick slices Italian-style bread

In a large, heavy skillet over medium heat brown beef cubes in oil. Pour off excess oil. Add pizza sauce and water. Stir to blend. Partially cover skillet; let mixture simmer for about 1 hour or until meat is tender. Add zucchini. Cook, stirring occasionally, until crisp-tender. Season with oregano. Serve over thick slices of Italian bread.

Makes 4 servings.

● DOUBLE-QUICK FRENCH-BREAD PIZZA WITH TOMATOES AND MUSHROOMS

4 slices from center of large, round French-style loaf (each slice about ½" thick)
Olive oil
8 tablespoons pizza sauce, homemade or canned
8 thin slices fresh tomato
8 large mushrooms, trimmed, sliced
1 tablespoon minced, fresh basil leaves or 1 teaspoon crumbled dried basil
1 teaspoon oregano leaves, crumbled
Salt and coarsely ground black pepper to taste
4 slices mozzarella or Swiss cheese

Preheat oven to 400° F. Brush each bread slice lightly with oil. Bake in preheated oven for 2 or 3 minutes. Top each slice with 2 tablespoons tomato sauce, tomato slices and mushrooms. Sprinkle with basil, oregano, salt and pepper. Cover each with a slice of cheese. Place in preheated oven and bake about 5 minutes until cheese is melted and bubbly.

Makes 2 servings.

● ENGLISH-MUFFIN PIZZAS

A quick fix for pizza lovers; the answer to making home-made pizza fun, quick and absolutely luscious. Yeasty English muffins are real winners for brunch, luncheon, supper or snacks.

ENGLISH-MUFFIN PIZZAS WITH MEXICAN-STYLE BEEF TOPPING

1 lb. ground beef
¼ lb. mushrooms, trimmed, coarsely chopped
1 small onion, peeled, chopped
2 small jalapeño chilis, peeled, seeded and finely chopped; or ¼ cup canned green chilis, seeded and finely chopped
½ teaspoon salt
3 English muffins, split to make 6 circles
2 tablespoons thick tomato sauce or ketchup

½ cup thinly sliced green onions, including green parts
½ cup slivered black olives
½ lb. shredded Monterey Jack cheese
1 medium-size ripe avocado
¼ cup grated Parmesan cheese
Sour cream for garnish, if desired
Mexican Salsa, if desired (see Chapter 4)

Cook beef in a large skillet over moderate heat, breaking up with a spoon or tip of spatula until no longer pink. Stir in mushrooms, onions and chilis. Cook 2 to 3 minutes, stirring constantly. Stir in tomato sauce or ketchup. Remove from heat.

Preheat oven to 450° F.

Remove the soft center from each English muffin circle (reserve for bread crumbs or other use). Place circles, flat side down, slightly apart on a long baking sheet. Spread meat mixture over each circle, dividing evenly. Scatter the green onions and olives over each. Cover each with a layer of shredded Monterey Jack cheese. Sprinkle with Parmesan cheese.

Bake in preheated oven for 10 minutes or until cheeses are melted.

Peel the avocado, remove and discard pit, and cut into very thin slices. Arrange over tops of pizzas. Garnish with sour cream and Mexican Salsa, if desired.

Makes 6 small pizzas.

ENGLISH-MUFFIN PEPPERONI PIZZAS

1 tablespoon olive or vegetable oil

8 oz. thinly sliced pepperoni

3 English muffins, split to make 6 circles

1 cup homemade pizza sauce or 1 8-oz. can pizza sauce

6 thin slices fontina cheese, cut into circles the same size as the English muffins

6 oz. shredded mozzarella cheese

Pour oil into large skillet over medium heat. When hot, add pepperoni slices, and sauté until lightly browned. Remove from skillet; drain.

Preheat oven to 450° F.

Remove the soft center from each English muffin circle (reserve for bread crumbs or other use). Place the circles, flat side down, slightly apart on a long, shallow baking sheet. Spread each with tomato sauce. Top with pepperoni slices, dividing evenly. Place a circle of fontina cheese over each and sprinkle with mozzarella.

Bake in preheated oven for 10 minutes or until cheese is melted.

Makes 6 small pizzas.

● FRIED PIZZA SANDWICHES

Another quick variation on the pizza theme.

4 thin slices mozzarella cheese
4 thin slices prosciutto
4 thin slices fontina cheese
8 slices firm white bread, crust
  removed
3 tablespoons butter

3 tablespoons olive oil
3 eggs, lightly beaten
¼ teaspoon dried basil
3 tablespoons water
1 2-oz. can rolled, caper-stuffed
  anchovy filets

Place 1 slice mozzarella cheese, 1 slice prosciutto and 1 slice fontina cheese between 2 slices of bread. Repeat, making 4 sandwiches; set aside. Place butter and olive oil in a large skillet over medium heat. In a bowl, beat eggs with basil and water until blended. Dip sandwich edges in egg mixture; press together. Dip both sides of sandwich in remaining egg mixture.

Fry 1 or 2 at a time in the hot butter-oil mixture until golden brown on both sides, turning once.

To serve, place each sandwich on a plate and top with anchovies.

Makes 4 servings.

● MIDDLE-EASTERN PITA PIZZA

2 pitas (Middle Eastern pocket
  bread)
8 tablespoons Garlic Lovers'
  Pizza Sauce (see Chapter 4)
  or pizza sauce of your
  preference

8 tablespoons crumbled feta
  cheese (about 2 oz.)
Mild California black olives, cut
  from stone into slivers
  (optional)

Preheat oven to 400° F.

One at a time, insert a small sharp knife into edge of pita and carefully slit entire edge. Use your hands to gently pull pita apart into 2 halves. One half will be hollow. Remove soft center from other half. Place the 4 halves cut side up on a flat baking sheet. Spoon 2 tablespoons pizza sauce into each. Top each with crumbled feta cheese and, if desired, olive slivers. Place in preheated oven and bake only until cheese is lightly melted and sauce bubbly hot.

Makes 2 servings.

● MEXICAN PIZZA

Easy as uno, dos, tres.

1 lb. ground beef
1 large onion, peeled, chopped
1 small green pepper, seeded, chopped
1 to 3 teaspoons chili powder, or to taste
1 6-oz. can tomato puree
Salt to taste
Coarsely ground black pepper to taste
Oil for frying tortilla

1 large flour tortilla (about 12½" in diameter)
4 to 6 large mushrooms, trimmed, thinly sliced
½ cup, chopped, pitted, black olives
½ cup chopped scallions with tops
4 oz. Monterey Jack cheese, shredded
2 oz. cheddar cheese, shredded

In a large skillet, brown meat in its own fat. Add onion and green pepper; cook and stir until vegetables are transparent. Stir in chili powder. Add tomato puree; cook and stir until sauce is bubbly hot. Season to taste with salt and pepper. Set aside.

Pour enough oil into a large, heavy skillet to come to a depth of about 1"; heat over medium-high heat until deep-fry thermometer registers 375° F. Fry tortilla in hot oil about 30 seconds on each side until golden brown. Remove with tongs to paper toweling to drain.

Heat broiler to high.

Place tortilla on pizza pan or baking sheet. Spread meat mixture evenly over surface. Sprinkle with mushrooms, black olives and scallions. Combine cheeses; sprinkle evenly over vegetables. Place under broiler until cheeses are melted, meat mixture bubbly hot. To serve, cut in half or into 4 wedges.

Makes 2 large or 4 small servings.

8

Pizza
Spin-Offs

Why certain flavors go together well is as mysterious to us as a formula in new math. Sour cream, chives and baked potatoes, for instance; molasses and mustard stirred into beans for baking; even eggs scrambled with crisp bacon. There are countless others. What we do know, however, is that combining a variety of pizza ingredients produces dishes that are a positive symphony of fragrant aroma, complementary textures, and compelling taste. Their fragrance in the house undoubtedly means that something particularly grand will soon appear on the table.

If you like pizza, you will love these recipes. Serve elegant, impressive Chicken Calzone as the featured entrée for a festive and formal dinner menu; treat a teenage crowd to hamburger pizzas; or present a fragrant pizza pot roast as a special treat for a family meal. Any one of them is sure to please. But then, so will the other pizza-inspired creations you will find here. They are all budget stretchers, quick and easy to prepare. We hope you will try each and every one of them. You'll find, as we did, they add great enjoyment and variety to meal planning all through the year.

● PIZZA AUBERGINE

Pizza with a difference! Crisp-fried crumb-coated eggplant forms the base for traditional pizza toppings.

1 medium eggplant
1 egg
1 tablespoon water
¾ cup commercial Italian-seasoned bread crumbs
¼ cup finely grated Parmesan cheese
¼ teaspoon coarsely ground black pepper
¼ teaspoon salt
½ cup flour
Oil for frying

1 cup tomato or pizza sauce, homemade or canned
6 thin slices mozzarella cheese
12 anchovy filets, drained, blotted dry
12 oil-cured Italian black olives, pitted, cut in halves
Chopped fresh basil or dried basil
Dried oregano
Olive oil

Peel and cut eggplant into thick slices (about ½" each). In a shallow bowl, beat egg with water. In a second shallow bowl, combine bread crumbs and grated cheese, pepper and salt. Spread flour out on waxed paper.

Dip eggplant slices in flour, then in beaten egg, and finally in seasoned bread crumbs, turning to coat both sides.

Pour enough oil into a deep, heavy skillet to come to about ½" in depth. Place over medium-high heat. When hot, add 2 or 3 of the eggplant slices and brown on both sides, turning once. Drain on paper towels. Fry remaining eggplant slices, adding additional oil if needed. Drain on paper towels and set aside.

Arrange broiler rack about 4" under source of heat. Pre-heat broiler.

Place prepared eggplant slices in single layer on a long, shallow baking sheet. Spread tomato sauce over each slice. Top each with a slice of mozzarella. Arrange anchovies and olive halves in an attractive design on top of cheese. Sprinkle with a little basil, oregano and olive oil. Place under broiler heat until cheese has melted. Serve at once.

Makes 6 eggplant pizzas, 3 to 6 servings.

●FILO DOUGH PIZZA PIE

Delicate filo leaves replace pizza crust to create a positively fabulous entrée.

1 10-oz. package frozen chopped spinach
¼ lb. butter (1 stick)
1 small bunch green onions, trimmed, coarsely chopped (about 1 cup)
1 clove garlic, peeled, minced
3 oz. mortadella or Italian salami, chopped
2 tablespoons fine, dry bread crumbs
2 eggs

1½ cups ricotta cheese
4 oz. fontina cheese, shredded
2 tablespoons grated Parmesan cheese
½ teaspoon mixed Italian herbs
Salt to taste
Pepper to taste
10 sheets filo dough, defrosted if frozen
½ cup additional fine, dry bread crumbs

Place frozen spinach in a colander until thoroughly defrosted. Press out all possible liquid. Set aside.

In a large skillet, melt butter over low heat. Remove all but 2 tablespoons and reserve this for the filo dough. Increase heat under skillet; when butter is bubbly, add onions and sauté until crisp-tender. Add garlic, well-drained spinach and mortadella or salami. Cook and stir until almost all excess liquid has been absorbed. Stir in 2 tablespoons bread crumbs and remove mixture from heat. Cool slightly; season with salt and pepper to taste.

In a large bowl, beat eggs until blended. Stir in ricotta cheese; mix thoroughly. Add fontina and Parmesan cheeses. Stir in spinach mixture; blend well. Set aside.

Preheat oven to 375° F.

Unfold the filo sheets on a flat work surface; cover lightly with plastic wrap, then with a slightly damp dish towel. Remove 1 sheet, leaving remainder covered. Place on a long, flat lightly buttered baking sheet. Brush evenly with melted butter; sprinkle lightly with about 1 tablespoon bread crumbs. Cover with second sheet of filo; brush with butter and sprinkle with more bread crumbs. Continue using 3 more sheets of dough, brushing each sheet with butter and sprinkling with crumbs. Spoon pizza filling onto center of last sheet in a rectangular shape, mounding slightly. Cover filling with another sheet of filo. Brush with butter; sprinkle lightly with bread crumbs. Add remaining sheets of dough, using most of remaining butter and all remaining bread crumbs on all but the last sheet. Fold long sides of dough toward center and fold in ends, enclosing filling completely. Brush top and sides of pie with remaining melted butter. Bake in preheated oven about 20 to 25 minutes until crust is golden brown.

Transfer pie to a serving platter; let cool about 5 minutes before cutting and serving.

Makes 4 servings.

● PIZZA-INSPIRED TOMATO SALAD

3 large, ripe tomatoes	2 tablespoons finely minced
4 thin slices mozzarella cheese	Italian parsley
4 thin slices Genoa salami	Italian Dressing (see recipe that
2 tablespoons chopped fresh	follows)
basil or ½ teaspoon dried	Niçoise olives
basil	

Cut tomatoes into thick slices, reserving ends for other use. Arrange, slightly overlapping, on a large serving platter with alternate slices of cheese and salami. Sprinkle with basil and parsley. Drizzle dressing over surface. Garnish with olives.

Makes 4 servings

ITALIAN DRESSING

4 tablespoons olive oil	½ teaspoon salt
1 tablespoon red wine vinegar	¼ teaspoon sugar
¼ teaspoon coarsely ground	
black pepper	

149

In a small bowl, combine ingredients and beat with a fork or whisk until thoroughly blended. Reblend, if necessary, just before using.

Makes sufficient dressing for Pizza-Inspired Tomato Salad.

● PIZZA-INSPIRED SEAFOOD

This pizza-inspired recipe evolved from an effort to use up the last of the "best ever" pizza sauce in our freezer.

2 small zucchini, trimmed, thinly sliced
½ lb. mushrooms, trimmed, coarsely chopped
1 small onion, peeled, chopped
1 small green pepper, seeded, thinly sliced
2 tablespoons olive oil
2 cups homemade pizza sauce or 1 1-lb. can pizza sauce
½ cup dry red wine

1 teaspoon dried oregano
¼ teaspoon ground sage
⅛ teaspoon coarsely ground black pepper
1 lb. peeled, deveined shrimp
½ lb. fresh fish filet
½ cup pimiento-stuffed olives, coarsely chopped
2 teaspoons capers, drained
4 thick slices Italian bread

In a large, heavy skillet over medium heat, cook zucchini, mushrooms, onion, and green pepper in olive oil until tender. Add pizza sauce, wine, herbs, and pepper. Simmer, uncovered, 15 to 20 minutes. Add shrimp, fish filets, olives and capers. Simmer only until shrimp are pink and filets firm and white. Serve over thick slices of Italian bread.

Makes 4 servings.

● PIZZA CHICKEN ROLL

1 whole chicken breast, boned but not skinned (see instructions that follow)
4 thin slices pepperoni

2 thin slices fontina cheese
4 or 5 pimiento-stuffed olives
2 tablespoons grated Parmesan cheese

Prepare chicken breast. Place on flat work surface. Cover with pepperoni and fontina cheese. Place olives in a row down center. Sprinkle with Parmesan cheese. Starting at one long side, roll chicken to encase filling completely.

Preheat oven to 400° F.

Place chicken roll seam side down, on a large sheet of heavy-duty foil on a flat baking sheet. Crimp edges of foil up. Bake in preheated oven for 30 minutes. Juices will form in foil.

Transfer chicken roll to serving platter. Spoon 1 to 2 teaspoons of juice over surface. Cool slightly. Cut into thick slices to serve.

Serves 4 as a main course, 8 as an appetizer.

HOW TO CUT UP A CHICKEN
(to obtain a whole chicken breast for stuffing)
Place chicken on one side on a flat surface. Move wing back and forth until joint pops up. Cut behind joint and remove wing. Repeat on other side. Place chicken breast-side up; pull leg away from body. Cut through skin and flesh to thigh joint. Press down until joint pops up. Cut leg-thigh section away from body. Repeat on other side. To remove lower back, cut between breast and back, slanting knife, until reaching rib bones. Break piece away through spinal column. Turn chicken breast-side down. Cut down along both sides of spinal column, removing it completely. Place breast skin-side down. With knife, cut through white cartilage at neck end of keel bone. Bend breast back, loosen keel bone by running thumb and index finger around both sides of bone and pull it out. Working one side at a time, insert tip of knife under long, narrow bone at wide portion of breast and remove. Insert knife under rib section and scrape it from meat. Reserve remaining chicken for other use.

● CHICKEN CALZONE

Whole boned chicken breasts stuffed with glorious pizza ingredients. Serve hot as an exciting entrée, or slice and serve at room temperature as part of an elegant Italian buffet.

1 whole chicken breast, boned but not skinned (see instructions that precede)
2 very thin slices Genoa salami, prosciutto or soppressata
2 tablespoons ricotta cheese, drained
1 teaspoon Pesto (see Chapter 4) or 1 teaspoon commercial pesto alla Genovese

1 teaspoon grated Parmesan cheese
2 tablespoons slivered, sharp, imported Italian provolone cheese

Prepare chicken breast. Place skin side down on work surface. Cover one half of breast with meat slices, leaving a ½″ border of uncovered chicken. Combine ricotta with pesto. Blend well. Spread over meat slices, leaving a ¼″ uncovered border. Sprinkle with remaining cheeses. Bring the uncovered portion of the chicken breast over filling. Roll edges of chicken meat and skin together. Secure firmly with small skewers, making sure stuffing is completely enclosed.

Preheat oven to 400° F.

Place calzone on heavy-duty foil on flat baking sheet. Crimp edges of foil up to catch chicken juice. Bake in preheated oven 30 to 35 minutes. Juices will accumulate in foil as chicken bakes. Transfer to serving platter. Spoon a few teaspoons of juice over surface. To serve, cut across into thick slices.

Makes 2 large or 4 small servings.

● PIZZA VEAL CHOPS

Serve these gloriously flavored chops with plenty of home-made pizza bread to mop up the sauce.

¼ cup flour
1 teaspoon salt
¼ teaspoon pepper
¼ teaspoon dried oregano
4 loin veal chops (about ½ lb. each)
2 tablespoons olive oil
2 tablespoons butter
¼ cup Marsala wine
1 cup homemade tomato sauce or 1 8-oz. can tomato sauce

1 small onion, peeled, thinly sliced, slices broken into rings
4 thick slices tomato
4 thin slices mozzarella or fontina cheese
8 flat anchovy filets, blotted dry; or 8 large, oil-cured black olives, pitted, cut into halves

In a shallow bowl, combine flour, salt, pepper and oregano. With your fingers spread each chop evenly with flour mixture; shake off excess, leaving only a thin film.

Heat oil and butter in a heavy skillet large enough to hold the chops in one layer. Add the chops, and cook, turning once, until lightly browned on both sides. Spoon off oil, then pour in wine and tomato sauce. Cover each chop with onion rings, dividing evenly. Place a tomato slice on top of each. Cover skillet, lower heat, and let simmer about 30 minutes until chops are tender. Cover each chop with a slice of cheese; criss-cross 2 anchovy filets over the top, or top with 4 olive halves. Cover skillet and continue to cook only until cheese has started to melt. Arrange chops on serving platter or plates. Spoon a little sauce over each; serve remaining sauce separately.

Makes 4 servings.

●HAMBURGER PIZZAS

A brilliant combination—two of America's favorite culinary creations come together.

2 lb. ground top round, top sirloin or other beef with about 20% to 25% fat

½ teaspoon salt

¼ teaspoon coarsely ground black pepper

⅛ teaspoon Italian seasoning

2 tablespoons peanut or vegetable oil

3 hamburger buns, each split in half

Olive oil

6 teaspoons grated Parmesan cheese

1 small red onion, peeled, thinly sliced, slices broken into rings

6 thick slices tomato

6 teaspoons additional grated Parmesan cheese

3 thin slices mozzarella cheese, cut into strips

1 cup homemade pizza sauce or 1 8-oz. can pizza sauce, heated

Place meat in a bowl, add salt, pepper and Italian seasonings. Mix with your hands, then shape into six round patties. Heat the peanut oil in a heavy skillet until hot but not smoking. Add patties and cook, turning once, about 4 minutes until lightly browned on both sides. Reduce heat and continue to cook about 2 minutes longer. Remove from skillet and set aside.

Place broiler rack about 4″ under heat. Preheat broiler.

Brush each half bun lightly with olive oil. Place, slightly apart, on a baking sheet. Sprinkle each with 1 teaspoon Parmesan cheese. Place under preheated broiler until lightly browned. Top each bun half with a hamburger patty. Cover each with a few onion rings, top with a tomato slice. Sprinkle with remaining Parmesan cheese. Cover with strips of mozzarella. Broil until cheeses are melted. Place on serving plates and spoon hot pizza sauce over each. Serve hot.

Makes 6 hamburger pizzas.

● PIZZA PORK ROAST

The aroma of this pizza-stuffed pork as it cooks is positively irresistible.

1 4-lb. boneless pork leg (fresh ham)

3 tablespoons butter

1 large onion, peeled, finely chopped

2 cloves garlic, peeled, minced

2 tablespoons finely minced parsley

4 tablespoons shredded mozzarella cheese

1 cup commercial Italian-seasoned bread crumbs

¼ teaspoon basil

¼ teaspoon oregano

¼ teaspoon marjoram

Salt

Pepper

1 egg

2 tablespoons grated Parmesan cheese

2 oz. very sharp provolone cheese, cut into slivers

2 tablespoons Marsala wine

2 tablespoons brown sugar

Preheat oven to 375° F.

Spread pork flat; pound with meat mallet to an even rectangle about 12" x 14".

Melt butter in a large, heavy skillet over low heat until foamy. When foaming begins to subside, add onion, garlic and parsley. Sauté until onion is tender. Scrape contents of skillet into a large mixing bowl. Cool slightly, then stir in mozzarella, bread crumbs, basil, oregano, marjoram, salt, pepper and egg. Spread mixture over flattened meat, leaving about a 1" border around all sides. Top with remaining cheeses. Starting with long side, gently roll meat, jelly roll fashion, enclosing filling completely. Fasten with metal skewers or tie together with butcher's cord. Wrap roll tightly in foil and place seam side down on rack in roasting pan.

Bake in preheated oven for 3 hours.

In a small saucepan, combine wine and sugar. Stir over low heat until sugar has dissolved.

155

Split top of foil on meat roast and fold down. Baste meat with wine mixture. Continue to roast, basting frequently, for about 30 minutes. Transfer roast to serving platter. Let stand about 5 minutes before slicing. Spoon pan juices over slices or serve pan juices separately.

Makes 6 to 8 servings.

9

Antipastos, Salads and Other Great Things to Serve with Pizza

If any entrée can be called a one-dish meal, it is a lusty and satisfying main-course pizza. With its contrasting flavors—rich, red tomatoes; assortment of cheeses; and abundant, zesty toppings—it is an Italian-style work of art, a food lover's celebration that needs little else for total perfection.

Nonetheless, to our way of thinking, a good meal, like a good story, needs an interesting introduction, an enticing first chapter to whet your appetite. Plus, of course, a happy ending.

Although most people insist that what they want with pizza is just more of the same, we've found that's not entirely true. When asked "But what about something to drink?" nine times out of ten the answer is "Oh, I forgot that—yes, I like wine" (or beer, or something else), in a tone indicating that a beverage is taken for granted. And then they often add, "Sometimes I like to start with a bit of salad." And when pressed they admit they often begin with an antipasto platter and, "well sometimes," end with a little light dessert with their espresso.

And so it goes. Even pizza, great as it is, needs some help to make a total meal. That is the reason for this chapter. It's a sampling of what goes with, before, and after pizza.

In our house, pizza party menus go something like this:

ANTIPASTO PLATTER

TWO PIZZAS MARGHERITA*
(each with a different assortment of toppings)
Italian Chianti
(or other dry, red wine)
ITALIAN ORANGE AND LEMON ICE*
Espresso
with imported Italian chocolates

or

PIZZA AMERICANA*
(plus another ready in the kitchen)
MAKE-AHEAD CAESAR SALAD*
Ice-cold beer
GRANITA DI CAFFEE*
with Italian amaretti cookies
Coffee with a splash of brandy

These are only suggested menus and not law. Pizza can also be served with only more pizza, and often we do just this—though we seldom serve it without some type of beverage and we do like to end with coffee plus, if nothing else, a few fresh grapes or strawberries when they are in season. But there we go, planning yet more pizza menus . . .

● ANTIPASTI

Antipasti can be as simple as paper-thin slices of prosciutto or soppressata wrapped around wedges of ripe melon, or as elaborate as an assortment of colorful oil-roasted and marinated vegetables garnished with anchovies or capers, interlaced with a variety of Italian sausages, cheeses and olives. Either way it is the perfect overture to a party-time pizza feast. You can make your cooking extra easy simply by opening an assortment of imported Italian cans, but with just a little more effort you can personalize and glorify your antipasto platter with any one of the following recipes. Their colors are more intense, their flavors more powerful than anything money can buy.

● EGGPLANT CUBES WITH ITALIAN HERBS

Spear each cube with a cocktail pick; serve with drinks or as part of your antipasto platter.

1 medium size eggplant (about 1 lb.)
Salt to taste
3 tablespoons olive oil
1 tablespoon red wine vinegar
1 tablespoon (or ¼ teaspoon if dried) of the following minced herbs: basil, thyme, rosemary, oregano

1 clove garlic, peeled, minced
Coarsely ground black pepper

Preheat oven to 350° F.

Wash eggplant, blot dry; trim ends but do not peel. Cut lengthwise in half, cut halves lengthwise into quarters. Cut quarters across into ½" cubes. Spread out on paper toweling, sprinkle evenly with salt. Let cubes stand about 15 minutes, turning them occasionally.

In a bowl, combine oil, vinegar, desired herbs, garlic and a light sprinkling of pepper. Add eggplant cubes, toss to coat evenly. Transfer cubes with a slotted spoon to a long, shallow baking dish just large enough to hold them in a single layer. Bake in preheated oven 25 to 30 minutes until tender. Cool to room temperature before serving.

Makes 6 to 10 servings.

● ROASTED ZUCCHINI AND YELLOW SQUASH

This ingenious Italian method of baking vegetables with oil and salt is positively fabulous; the salt draws out excess moisture and intensifies flavors while the oil keeps the vegetables from drying out.

4 to 6 very small yellow squash   ½ to 2 tablespoons salt, prefer-
4 to 6 very small zucchini   ably coarse (kosher) variety
Approximately ⅓ cup olive oil

Preheat oven to 350° F.

Wash vegetables, blot dry; do not trim. Arrange them closely together in a long, shallow baking dish just large enough to hold them in a single layer. Pour a thin film of oil over each; sprinkle generously with salt. Bake about 30 minutes until vegetables are almost limp and lightly browned. Drain. Bring to room temperature, then cut into bite-size chunks or thick slices. Serve at room temperature.

Makes 6 to 10 servings.

●WINTER VEGETABLE SALAD FOR ANTIPASTO PLATTER

1 10-oz. package frozen corn
kernels, cooked according to
package directions, drained
1 6-oz. jar marinated artichoke
hearts, chopped, and their
marinade
2 tablespoons white wine
vinegar

½ teaspoon dried oregano
Salt to taste
Romaine lettuce, or spinach
leaves
Grated Parmesan cheese

In a large bowl, combine corn, artichoke hearts and their marinade, vinegar, oregano and salt. Toss to mix. Refrigerate until chilled or until ready to serve.

To serve on an antipasto platter, spoon about 1 tablespoon of salad onto a crisp lettuce or spinach leaf. Sprinkle lightly with grated cheese. Roll up and spear with cocktail picks.

Makes 6 to 10 servings.

●MARINATED VEGETABLES ITALIAN-STYLE

Serve with your pizza or before; solo or as part of an elaborate antipasto creation.

½ cup white wine vinegar
½ teaspoon sugar
¼ teaspoon coarsely ground
black pepper
¼ teaspoon salt

¾ cup olive or mild vegetable
oil
1 clove garlic, peeled, finely
chopped
2 carrots, scraped, thinly sliced

2 cups cauliflower flowerets

1 cup broccoli flowerets

1 cup trimmed, thinly sliced, broccoli stems

3 to 4 stalks celery, thinly sliced on the diagonal

2 tablespoons capers, well drained

Prepare marinade: place vinegar, sugar, pepper and salt in a large bowl. Beat with whisk until sugar has dissolved. Stir in olive or vegetable oil and garlic; set aside.

Bring a large pot of water to a full boil. Drop in carrot slices, let boil only until crisp-tender. Remove from water with a small sieve or slotted spoon, drain briefly, then add to bowl of marinade. Repeat, one at a time, with remaining vegetables. Stir each into the marinade while still hot. Stir in capers. Cool to room temperature, then cover and refrigerate for 12 to 24 hours. Drain off marinade just before serving vegetables as an accompaniment to your pizza or as part of a first-course antipasto.

Makes 6 to 10 servings.

● GREEN BEAN SALAD

Here is another vegetable that can be served along with your pizza or as part of an antipasto.

1 lb. green beans

½ teaspoon salt

Olive oil

Lemon juice, salt and pepper, to taste

Snip both ends off beans, pulling away any possible strings.

Bring a large pot of water to a full boil; add about ½ teaspoon salt. When water has come to a full boil, drop in beans. When water has returned to boil, reduce heat and let beans cook at a brisk simmer until tender. Very young beans may take 6 to 7 minutes while larger, older ones may require up to 10 minutes. Start testing after about 6 minutes. When crisp-tender, drain into a colander and then rinse immediately under cold running water to stop cooking process. Transfer to a large bowl. Add just enough olive oil to coat each bean; then add lemon juice, salt and pepper to taste. Bring to room temperature before serving. If made ahead, bring beans to room temperature then cover and refrigerate until about 1 hour before serving. They taste best if not overchilled.

Makes 6 to 10 servings.

● CAULIFLOWER SALAD WITH CAPERS

Mild cauliflower is brought to zesty life with capers.

2 cups cauliflower flowerets
Salt
Olive oil

Red wine vinegar
2 to 3 tablespoons capers, drained

Bring a large pot of salted water to full boil; drop in flowerets and bring back to full boil. Reduce heat slightly, let flowerets cook about 4 minutes only until crisp-tender. Drain into a colander, then rinse immediately under cold running water to stop cooking process. Transfer flowerets to a large bowl; add sufficient olive oil to coat them lightly. Sprinkle with vinegar; toss briefly, add capers. Serve at room temperature.

Makes 6 to 10 servings.

● ITALIAN SALAD WITH MARINATED ARTICHOKE HEARTS

1 small bunch broccoli
2 large carrots, scraped and
  sliced into thin rounds
1 lb. fresh spinach or 1 10-oz.
  package fresh spinach,
  washed, trimmed, and torn
  into bite-size pieces
6 to 8 scallions, washed,
  trimmed, cut across into
  rings

1 large cucumber, peeled,
  halved lengthwise, seeded,
  and cut into half moon pieces
1 small jar Italian-style marinated artichoke hearts
1 small can chick-peas, drained
  and rinsed

Cut stems from broccoli, break tops into small flowerets, trim stems, cut lengthwise into thin slices, cut slices into ½ lengths.

Fill a large saucepan with water and bring to a full boil over high heat. Add broccoli stems, let boil 3 to 4 minutes, add broccoli flowerets and carrots. Continue to boil until vegetables are crisp-tender; drain into a colander, then place immediately under cold running water to stop the cooking process and retain colors. Blot thoroughly dry. Place in a large salad bowl. Add spinach, green onions, and cucumber. Drain artichoke hearts, retain marinade for dressing. Add to vegetables in bowl. Add chick-peas and toss to blend all ingredients.

Pour dressing over vegetable mixture just before serving; toss well and serve at room temperature.

Makes 6 to 8 servings.

DRESSING

Marinade from artichoke hearts
2 tablespoons white wine vinegar
2 tablespoons fresh lemon juice
1 teaspoon dried oregano
2 teaspoons minced fresh
   thyme or ¼ teaspoon dried
   thyme

Olive or vegetable oil, as needed
Freshly ground black pepper
Pinch of sugar
Salt to taste

Combine ingredients in large bowl and beat with a whisk until thoroughly blended, or place in work bowl of food processor, cover and process until blended.

● CRISP-COOKED VEGETABLE SALAD WITH MUSTARD VINAIGRETTE

1 small bunch broccoli
1 small head cauliflower
½ lb. fresh green beans,
   trimmed, cut into 1" pieces
2 medium carrots, scraped,
   very thinly sliced
1 green pepper, seeded, cut
   into 1" strips

1 head romaine lettuce, or 1
   large bunch fresh spinach
   leaves, washed, trimmed,
   tough stems removed, leaves
   torn into bite-size pieces
6 to 8 small radishes, trimmed,
   very thinly sliced

Cut stems from broccoli; break tops into small flowerets, trim stems, cut lengthwise into narrow strips, then across into ½" lengths. Place flowerets and stems in a large bowl of heavily salted cold water. Set aside. Trim cauliflower, cut into small flowerets; add to broccoli in ice water. Bring a large pot of water to a full boil, drain and add broccoli and cauliflower; boil for 1 to 2 minutes or until crisp-tender. Remove vegetables from boiling water with a small sieve and transfer them to a colander. Immediately rinse under cold running water to stop the cooking process. Add green beans, carrots and green pepper strips to the boiling water; boil 1 to 2 minutes or until crisp-tender. Drain into colander and rinse under cold running water, to stop the cooking process and preserve color. Blot all vegetables completely dry and transfer them to a large bowl; set aside.

Pour dressing over cooked vegetables. Refrigerate until well chilled or until ready to serve. Drain dressing into a separate bowl.

Line a bowl with romaine lettuce or spinach leaves and top with the marinated vegetables. Garnish with radish slices. Serve the dressing poured from the vegetables separately.

Makes 6 to 8 servings.

MUSTARD VINAIGRETTE

1/4 cup white wine vinegar
2 tablespoons Dijon mustard (or similar prepared mustard)
3/4 cup mild vegetable oil
2 teaspoons chopped fresh basil or 1/2 teaspoon dried basil
2 teaspoons chopped fresh tarragon leaves or 1/2 teaspoon dried tarragon

1/2 teaspoon chopped fresh thyme or sprinkling of dried thyme
1/2 teaspoon sugar
Salt to taste
Freshly ground black pepper to taste

In a bowl mix vinegar with mustard until smooth. Add oil in a slow, steady stream, beating with whisk as added. Stir in basil, tarragon, thyme and sugar. Season to taste with salt and pepper.

●NAPA CABBAGE SALAD

This salad is typically American because its ingredients are of mixed nationalities. It evolved from a marked dislike of wilted and worn-out imported lettuce, the only kind available at the market one year.

1 small or ½ large Napa (Chinese) cabbage (enough to make about 3 cups shredded cabbage)
1 6-oz. jar Italian-style marinated artichoke hearts
1 large navel orange
1 small avocado
Oil (optional)
White wine vinegar (optional)
Salt and coarsely ground black pepper to taste

Trim cabbage and cut across with a sharp knife into very fine shreds; place in a large bowl. Pour marinade from artichoke hearts over cabbage, then coarsely chop the hearts and add them to the bowl. Using a small, sharp knife, cut orange into quarters. Cut quarters into thick wedges. Holding wedges over bowl, cut fruit from peel into bowl. Cut avocado in half, peel halves, cut lengthwise into thin slices; add to cabbage mixture. Toss to blend. If desired, add oil or vinegar or both, depending on whether you like your salad tart or mild. Season to taste with salt and pepper.

Makes 6 servings.

Note: Napa (Chinese) cabbage is a tall, tightly packed, fresh cabbage with wide, white stalks and light green, crinkly leaves.

● BEAUTIFUL UGLI FRUIT AND AVOCADO SALAD

If you haven't experienced the beautiful flavor of ugli fruit you're in for a delightful surprise; the flavor is a cross between orange and grapefruit yet distinctly its own.

1 large ugli fruit	Parsley Vinaigrette (see recipe
1 large or 2 medium ripe	that follows)
avocados	Crisp lettuce leaves

Peel ugli fruit with a sharp knife to remove both the rind and the white skin. Hold the fruit over a bowl to catch the juice and cut between the membrances to remove each section, letting them drop into the bowl. Remove any seeds. Cut avocado in half, remove pit and peel each half. Cut halves lengthwise into wedges. Add Parsley Vinaigrette and toss to blend. Cover and refrigerate until ready to use. When ready to serve, drain and arrange ugli fruit sections and avocado wedges over crisp lettuce leaves on individual salad plates. Spoon a little of the dressing left in the bowl over each serving.

Serve remaining dressing separately.

Makes 4 to 6 servings.

PARSLEY VINAIGRETTE

1 tablespoon minced parsley	1 teaspoon lemon juice
1 tablespoon finely chopped	1/8 teaspoon dry mustard
chives	Salt and coarsely ground black
2 tablespoons white wine	pepper to taste
vinegar	1/4 cup olive oil

Combine ingredients in work bowl of food processor or blender; blend until smooth. Or place ingredients in a large mixing bowl and beat with a whisk until blended.

• INSALATA DI CAVOLFIORE

(Cauliflower Salad)

This classic Italian salad can be served as part of an anti-pasto platter or an accompaniment to pizza or any other Italian-style (or for that matter any style) meal.

1 medium cauliflower
1 2-oz. flat tin anchovy filets
  packed in olive oil
1 to 2 tablespoons white wine
  vinegar or fresh lemon juice

¼ cup finely minced parsley
  (Italian parsley preferred)
Freshly ground black pepper to
  taste

Trim cauliflower and break into flowerets. Add to a large pot of rapidly boiling salted water; boil about 2 minutes until crisp-tender. Drain immediately into a colander, rinse under cold running water to stop cooking process. Place in a large bowl.

Pour the oil from the anchovies over the cauliflower. Coarsely chop anchovies and add them to the bowl. Stir in vinegar or lemon juice; add minced parsley and pepper. Toss to blend. Taste and, if desired, add a little more vinegar or lemon juice.

Let salad stand for about 1 hour to blend flavors before serving. Serve at room temperature.

Makes 6 servings.

● MAKE-AHEAD CAESAR SALAD

We're told this salad was created at Caesar's Bar and Grill in Tijuana, Mexico, just south of the border near the fragrant orange groves of California. It was made by Caesar himself, so they say, on the spur of the moment with whatever was available in his kitchen. This version was created much the same way and we're told it is every bit as delicious as the original.

½ cup mild salad oil
¼ cup white wine vinegar
2 teaspoons Worcestershire
  sauce
Dash Tabasco sauce
¼ teaspoon sugar
¼ teaspoon salt
Sprinkling of coarsely ground
  black pepper
1 clove garlic, peeled,
  crushed

1 medium head romaine
  lettuce, washed, blotted
  dry, torn into bite-size
  pieces
¼ cup grated Parmesan cheese
1 oz. crumbled blue cheese
1½ cups croutons, made from
  Basic Pizza Bread (see Chapter 2) or commercial Italian-
  seasoned croutons
1 egg

In a small bowl, combine, oil, vinegar, Worcestershire sauce, Tabasco sauce, sugar, salt and pepper. Beat with a whisk until well blended. Add garlic. Cover and refrigerate several hours to blend flavors.

Place lettuce in a large salad bowl. Sprinkle with cheese and croutons. Remove crushed garlic from dressing; add egg and beat until well blended. Pour over salad, toss to blend. Serve immediately.

Makes 6 to 8 servings.

● GUACAMOLE SALAD

Great to serve with Mexican Pizza, but just as good with any pizza you care to serve.

1 large ripe tomato
3 large avocados
2 tablespoons lemon juice
1/4 teaspoon salt
6 to 8 green onions, trimmed, thinly sliced, green part included
2 small jalapeño chilis, peeled, seeded, finely chopped; or 1/4 cup canned green chilis, seeded, finely chopped

1 tablespoon finely minced Italian parsley
1/4 teaspoon dried cumin (optional)
Dash Tabasco sauce
Crisp lettuce leaves (optional)

Cut tomato in half, gently squeeze out seeds and juice. Cut halves into thin strips. Blot dry. Set aside.

Peel, pit and mash avocado in a medium-size bowl. Stir in tomato strips, lemon juice, salt, green onions, chilis and parsley. If desired, stir in cumin. Season with Tabasco sauce. Blend well. Cover; chill several hours. Serve on crisp lettuce leaves, if desired.

Makes 4 to 6 servings.

● CRISP SALAD WITH WALNUTS AND FRESH LEMON VINAIGRETTE

This simple, light but very flavorful lettuce salad is the perfect choice to serve before or after a main-course deep-dish or Sicilian-style pizza.

1 large head leaf lettuce or Boston lettuce
½ cup finely chopped walnuts

Fresh Lemon Vinaigrette (see recipe that follows)

Trim damaged leaves from lettuce and discard; remove core. Tear leaves into bite-size pieces. Drop leaves into a sink filled with cold water and swish them around with your hands; any sand or dirt will fall to the bottom. Lift leaves out of the water and place on a double-thickness of paper towels; roll up loosely. Place roll in crisper in refrigerator for about 30 minutes; the paper towels will drain off all moisture. Place dry leaves in a large salad bowl, add the walnuts and fresh Lemon Vinaigrette. Toss to blend thoroughly, and serve at once.

Makes 4 to 6 servings.

FRESH LEMON VINAIGRETTE

4 tablespoons mild salad oil
2 tablespoons fresh lemon juice
½ teaspoon salt

¼ teaspoon sugar
Coarsely ground black pepper to taste

Combine all ingredients in small bowl and beat with whisk until well blended. Let stand at room temperature until ready to use. Pour over greens and toss just before serving.

Pizza Dolce, and Desserts to Complete a Pizza Feast

Pizza for dessert? Why yes, of course. You'll find recipes for it in most authentic Italian cookbooks, both old and new. Although pizza in Italy simply means pie, *pizza dolce* is most frequently made in that country with raised yeast dough that is shaped big, round, and flat, then covered with a sweet topping, or made into sweetly filled calzones or pizza turnovers. Both are quite special.

In the pages that follow, you'll find a few recipes for authentic *pizza dolce*, plus a number of easy adaptations. They all look positively beautiful and taste sensational. In fact, elegant is not too strong a word to describe them. They are, indeed, impressive—and, though it's hard to believe, they are quick and easy to make. They are so simple to prepare, in fact, that a great new entertaining idea is beginning to catch on in this country. It's the dessert pizza party: an entertaining alternative for anything from "cocktails and hors d'oeuvres" to a four-course formal dinner.

A beautiful, sweet pizza creation is a festive way to treat your friends after the theater, after the "game," or after anything. But you don't need a special occasion. Glamorous pizza desserts are made for good times, anytime.

CALZONE DOLCE WITH RICOTTA FILLINGS

Beautiful and incredibly delicious—yet surprisingly quick to prepare. A rich, creamy, smooth ricotta filling and commercial frozen puff-pastry dough are the secrets of its success.

Desired ricotta filling (see recipes that follow)
1 sheet commercial frozen puff pastry, from 1 17¼-oz. package

1 egg white, lightly beaten

Preheat oven to 425° F.

Prepare filling; set aside.

Thaw puff pastry sheet for 20 minutes, then unfold. Roll out on a lightly floured surface to a 14" x 15" rectangle. Cut points of rectangle to form an oval so that filling will fit in corners when dough is folded over. Brush edges of dough with egg white. Place flat baking sheet lengthwise in front of you; arrange half of long side of pastry on center of sheet, leaving other half overlapping sheet. Mound desired filling on half of dough on sheet, leaving ½" border. Fold other half of dough over to form turnover, pressing edges together with fingers to seal. With tines of fork flute decoratively. Brush top evenly with egg white. Make 3 steam vents with tip of knife.

Bake 25 to 30 minutes or until puffed and golden brown. Let stand at room temperature about 5 minutes before cutting and serving.

Makes 4 to 6 servings.

Note: This not-too-sweet Italian creation with its French accent of puff pastry is a wonderful replacement for Danish or croissants at breakfast, delightful with afternoon tea, and the perfect accompaniment to chilled white wine.

RICOTTA FILLING WITH CREAM SHERRY

2 cups ricotta cheese
1 egg yolk
¼ cup sugar

1 teaspoon cream sherry
1½ oz. raisins

In a bowl, combine ricotta cheese, egg yolk, sugar, sherry and raisins. Beat until well blended. Set aside until ready to use.

NEAPOLITAN-STYLE RICOTTA FILLING

2 cups ricotta cheese
½ cup confectioner's sugar
2 tablespoons finely minced candied orange peel or citron
3 tablespoons grated semi-sweet chocolate

2 tablespoons Marsala wine, cream sherry or orange liqueur

In a large bowl, combine ingredients. Blend well.

PIZZA DESSERT PARTY

SWEET PIZZAS WITH APRICOT AND RICOTTA FILLING*

MARSHMALLOW-CHOCOLATE CALZONE*
(still slightly warm from the oven)

Make-your-own sundaes
(assorted ice creams, raspberry sauce, slivered almonds, chopped pecans, slivered chocolate, fresh strawberries, and whipped cream)

Coffee

● FESTIVE SWEET PIZZA DOUGH

Part of the pleasure of eating a dessert pizza should be the delight of a bite of the crust. This slightly sweet buttery yeast dough, made with wine or sherry instead of water, will live up to your highest expectations.

1 package dry yeast	4 tablespoons butter, chilled
1/8 teaspoon sugar	1 egg, room temperature
1/2 cup warm water (105° to 110° F)	6 tablespoons Marsala or Madeira wine or cream sherry
3 cups all-purpose flour	sherry
2 tablespoons additional sugar	Additional water, as needed
1/2 teaspoon salt	Additional flour, as needed

Hand Method: Place yeast in a 1-cup measure; add 1/8 teaspoon sugar and water. Let stand until yeast has dissolved and mixture is bubbly. Place flour, salt and remaining sugar in a large mixing bowl. Cut butter into small slivers and work into the flour mixture until butter is no longer discernible and mixture resembles coarse oatmeal. In a small bowl, beat egg with wine or sherry. Add to yeast mixture, blend, then stir into flour mixture. Mix to a soft dough that will pull away from sides of bowl. If too dry, sprinkle with a little more water. Turn out on a lightly floured work surface and sprinkle with a little additional flour. Press dough down with heel of your hand, then knead until smooth and elastic, adding more flour if necessary to keep dough from sticking to surface. Form into a smooth ball.

Processor Method: Place yeast in a 1-cup measure, add 1/8 teaspoon sugar and the water. Let stand until yeast has dissolved and mixture is bubbly. Spoon the flour, salt and remaining sugar into work bowl of food processor. Turn the motor on and off several times to mix ingredients. Remove the processor cover; holding butter over the bowl, cut it into thin slivers, letting them fall into the flour mixture. Cover processor, turn motor on and off several times until butter is mixed with flour. In a bowl, beat egg with wine or sherry. Add to yeast mixture, blend well; pour mixture through feed tube of processor. Process until dough leaves sides of work bowl and forms into 1 or 2 soft balls on processor blades.

Turn dough out on a lightly floured work surface; sprinkle surface lightly with flour, then knead 2 to 3 minutes or until dough is smooth and elastic, adding additional flour if dough sticks to work surface. Shape into a smooth ball.

Place ball of dough in a lightly floured bowl, turn to coat evenly. Cover bowl with plastic wrap and let stand in a warm, draft-free place about 1½ hours until dough is double in volume.

When dough has doubled in volume, turn it out on a lightly floured work surface. Sprinkle lightly with flour, then flatten with your hands. Using a rolling pin, roll dough out into a 12″ to 14″ circle, turning it occasionally as it is rolled and spreading lightly with flour if necessary. Fold circle into quarters, center the point in a 12″ or 14″ pizza pan, unfold to cover pan and press up to cover sides of pan. Fill, top and bake as directed in individual recipes.

SWEET PIZZA WITH BRANDIED FRUIT
Great to serve instead of the usual bake-shop Danish for a festive late breakfast or brunch.

1 6-to-7-oz. package mixed
   dried fruits
Water
¼ cup applejack or other
   brandy
Festive Sweet Pizza Dough, or
   All-Purpose Pizza Dough for
   one 12″ to 14″ round pizza
   (see Chapter 3)

¼ cup sugar
½ pint whipping cream

Place fruit in a saucepan and cover by about 1″ with water. Simmer over low heat about 30 minutes until fruit is tender. Drain. Place in a bowl and add brandy. Cover and refrigerate up to 2 days or until ready to use.

Prepare pizza dough. Set aside to rise.

While dough rises, bring fruit mixture to room temperature. Drain into a colander set over a bowl. Reserve liquid in bowl for topping. Chop fruit into small pieces.

Preheat oven to 425° F.

When dough has risen, punch down and turn out on a floured work surface. Knead, then flour and shape in pizza pan as directed.

Cover dough with chopped fruit. Sprinkle fruit evenly with sugar. Bake pizza in preheated oven until crust is lightly browned.

Beat cream until stiff, fold in reserved brandy.

To serve, cut warm pizza into wedges and top each with dollops of the whipped cream mixture.

Makes one 12" to 14" round pizza.

WINTER FRUIT PIZZA

This pizza makes such an astonishingly beautiful dessert you won't believe it until you see it yourself.

Festive Sweet Pizza Dough, or All-Purpose Pizza Dough for one 12" to 14" round pizza (see Chapter 3)

½ stick very cold, firm butter (4 tablespoons)

2 tablespoons sugar

1 1-lb. can pitted red cherries, drained, blotted thoroughly dry

1 1-lb. can pear or peach halves, drained, blotted thoroughly dry

1 1-lb. can pineapple chunks, drained, blotted thoroughly dry

2 tablespoons additional sugar

Prepare pizza dough. Let rise until volume doubles.

Preheat oven to 425° F.

When dough has risen, punch down and turn out on a floured work surface. Sprinkle lightly with flour. Flatten into a disk, then with floured rolling pin roll out, turning dough occasionally and spreading lightly with flour until it becomes a thin circle just slightly larger than the pan you are going to use. Transfer the circle to a 12" or 14" pizza pan. Turn edges under and crimp with your fingers against sides of pan.

Holding the stick of butter in one hand over dough, with a sharp knife cut about half of it into thin slivers, letting the slivers fall evenly over dough. Sprinkle evenly with 2 tablespoons sugar. Cover center of dough with cherries, surround them with pear or peach halves, then cover remaining dough with pineapple chunks. Sliver remaining butter evenly over fruit and sprinkle with remaining sugar.

Bake in preheated oven until crust is lightly browned, fruit well glazed. Remove pizza from oven and let stand 15 to 20 minutes to allow juices to thicken before slicing.

Makes 6 to 8 servings.

PEACHY PIZZA COFFEE CAKE
You'll be pleased when you see this sweet pizza dough rise to a soft, tender coffee cake, and extra pleased when you turn it right-side-up and discover its beautiful topping.

Festive Sweet Pizza Dough
3 tablespoons butter
½ cup light brown sugar
½ cup walnut halves

4 to 6 large ripe peaches, peeled and sliced; or 1 1-lb. can sliced cling peaches, drained, blotted thoroughly dry

Prepare pizza dough. Set aside to rise.

Preheat oven to 425° F.

Let butter stand at room temperature until soft; spread evenly over bottom of a 12" pizza pan. Sprinkle butter evenly with sugar. Arrange walnut halves and peach slices in an attractive design over sugar.

When dough has risen, punch down and turn out onto a lightly floured work surface. Sprinkle lightly with flour, flatten with your hands into a disk about 1" thick. Roll disk into a circle just a little larger than the pan. Place over walnut halves and sliced peaches, turning excess dough back around edge of pan. Bake in preheated oven 15 to 20 minutes. Remove from oven, place on rack and let stand about 15 minutes. Place a large round platter over pizza pan and, holding pan and platter together firmly, invert pizza onto platter and remove pan.

Makes one 12" coffee cake pizza.

181

● MARSHMALLOW-CHOCOLATE CALZONE

The ultimate sweet pizza dessert, fantastic and utterly irresistible from first look to last bite. Fantastically easy to prepare, too.

1 6-oz. package chocolate chips
6 tablespoons miniature
 marshmallows
2 tablespoons shredded
 coconut

1 package frozen commercial
 puff-pastry shells (6 shells)
2 tablespoons butter

In a bowl, combine 6 tablespoons chocolate chips, the marshmallows and coconut; set aside.

Let puff pastry shells stand at room temperature until softened slightly but still cold. One at a time, roll each out into a 6″ to 7″ circle. Place about 1 tablespoon of chocolate-marshmallow mixture in center of one half of circle. With your fingers, dampen edges of dough with cold water. Fold uncovered portion of dough over filling and press edges together to seal. Flute with tines of a fork. Place as prepared on flat surface in freezer. When all are prepared, freeze about 30 minutes until firm.

Preheat oven to 400° F.

Place remaining chocolate chips in the top half of a double boiler over simmering water. Add butter and stir until chocolate has melted to a smooth sauce. Let stand over hot water until ready to use.

Place frozen calzones, slightly apart, on a long, flat baking sheet. Bake about 15 minutes until puffed and lightly browned. Place on dessert plates, top with hot chocolate sauce and serve at once.

Makes 6 sweet calzones.

●CARAMELIZED APPLE PIZZA WITH SHARP CHEDDAR CHEESE

Straight from a deluxe California restaurant. A simply beautiful, fantastically flavorful and extra festive pizza dessert.

8 to 10 tart, crisp cooking apples
1 teaspoon lemon juice
2 cups water
3 cups additional water
1 cup sugar
1 stick cinnamon, broken into several pieces
6 whole cloves
1 vanilla bean or 1 teaspoon vanilla extract
Zest (yellow part of peel) from one small lemon, cut into julienne strips

2 cups additional sugar
2 tablespoons butter
1 tablespoon lemon juice
1 tablespoon apple brandy or applejack
1 sheet commercial frozen puff pastry from 1 17¼-oz. package frozen puff pastry
1 teaspoon grated nutmeg
½ cup sharp cheddar cheese, shredded or finely crumbled

Peel and core each apple, cut into quarters, cut quarters into thin slices and drop as sliced into a large bowl of icy cold lemon water (about 1 teaspoon lemon juice to 2 cups water). Set aside until ready to use.

In a large saucepan, combine 3 cups water, 1 cup sugar, cinnamon, cloves, vanilla and lemon zest. Place over medium heat and stir until sugar dissolves. Let simmer about 10 minutes. Add apples and simmer about 5 minutes, only until crisp-tender. Transfer apples with a slotted spoon to a colander; set aside. (Reserve cooking syrup for another use. It's great over fried pizza or pancakes). Place remaining 2 cups sugar in a large, heavy skillet. Cook, stirring constantly, over medium heat until sugar has dissolved to a deep golden syrup. Pour immediately into a 12″ round pizza pan and quickly tilt pan back and forth to spread syrup evenly to edges. Syrup will harden to a brittle glaze.

183

Remove apple slices from lemon water and blot dry; arrange in overlapping circles in pizza pan, covering glaze completely.

Preheat oven to 425° F.

Let frozen puff pastry stand at room temperature for about 20 minutes to soften. Unfold on floured work surface, roll out to a 14" square. With a sharp knife cut off points of square to form a circle; place over apples in pan, fold edges under to seal in apples and glaze, covering pan completely.

Bake in preheated oven 30 to 35 minutes or until crust is puffed and brown. Remove from oven and let stand about 10 minutes. Place a large, round platter (14" or larger) or flat baking sheet directly on top of pizza and, holding pizza pan and platter or baking sheet together firmly, invert pizza onto platter or baking sheet and remove pan. Sprinkle evenly with nutmeg and shredded or crumbled cheese. Cut into wedges and serve warm.

Makes one large pizza (8 servings).

● SWEET APPLE PIZZAS WITH ALMONDS

Beautiful to look at and utterly delicious. Brew up some espresso and enjoy!

6 large crisp apples
1 tablespoon lemon juice
2 cups water
¼ cup brown sugar
1 cup additional water
1 10-oz. package frozen
   commercial puff-pastry shells
   (6 shells)

1 cup slivered almonds
Cinnamon and confectioner's
   sugar to taste

Peel, core and cut apples into thin slices, drop as sliced into a large bowl of icy lemon water (1 tablespoon lemon juice to 2 cups water). When all are peeled and sliced, drain and transfer them to a saucepan, add sugar and water. Place over low heat and let simmer uncovered for about 10 minutes, stirring occasionally. Remove apples with a slotted spoon and set aside. Discard cooking syrup.

Let puff pastry shells stand at room temperature until softened slightly but still cold. One at a time, roll each out into a 6″ to 7″ circle. Turn up edges of each circle to form small rims. Place on a flat surface in freezer. When all are prepared, place, slightly apart, on a flat baking sheet.

Preheat oven to 400° F. Cover each shaped pastry circle with apple slices, arranging them in an attractive design. Sprinkle each with slivered almonds, dividing evenly. Top with cinnamon and confectioner's sugar. Bake in preheated oven 20 to 25 minutes or until pastry is lightly browned and puffed. Serve warm or at room temperature.

Makes 6 small dessert pizzas.

● SWEET PIZZAS WITH APRICOT AND RICOTTA FILLING

So elegant, so festive, no one will believe they were so easy to prepare.

1 cup ricotta cheese
¼ cup sugar
1 tablespoon apricot brandy or
   cream sherry
6 tablespoons currant jelly

1 15-oz. can apricot halves
1 10-oz. package frozen commercial puff-pastry shells (6 shells)

In a bowl, combine cheese, sugar, brandy or sherry. Blend well. Set aside. Place jelly in top half of double boiler over simmering water until melted. Let stand over hot water until ready to use. (If jelly thickens before ready to use, reheat until remelted.) Drain apricot halves into a bowl. (Reserve juice for other use.)

Let puff pastry shells stand at room temperature until softened slightly but still cold. One at a time, roll each out into a 6" to 7" circle. Turn up edges of each circle to form small rims. Place on a flat surface in freezer. When all are prepared, place, slightly apart, on a flat baking sheet.

Preheat oven to 400° F.

Spoon ricotta filling into each shell, dividing evenly. Spread out with back of a spoon to cover pastry completely. Top each with apricot halves, covering filling completely. Spoon about 1 tablespoon of melted currant jelly over each.

Bake in preheated oven until crust is lightly browned and puffed. Serve warm or at room temperature.

Makes 6 small dessert pizzas.

● WALNUT-CARAMEL PIZZA WITH CHOCOLATE GLAZE

An extravagance of crisp buttery crust, caramelized walnuts and bittersweet chocolate.

Butter for pan
2¾ cups flour
¼ cup sugar
4 tablespoons water
1 egg white, beaten until frothy
1 cup firmly packed brown sugar
¼ cup white cane syrup
¼ cup water

¾ cup butter (1½ sticks), chilled, cut into small cubes
2 egg yolks
2 cups chopped walnuts
¼ cup butter
4 oz. bittersweet chocolate (4 squares)
2 tablespoons butter

Preheat oven to 425°. Butter a 12" to 14" pizza pan.

In a large bowl combine flour and sugar. Add butter cubes.

With pastry blender or fingers work until mixture resembles coarse meal.

In a small bowl beat egg yolks with water. Add to flour mixture and blend well. Form into ball. Refrigerate until chilled.

On a floured board roll out dough to 14" to 15" circle. Fit into pizza pan. Flute edges between thumb and second finger to form decorative rim. Cover bottom of dough with foil, shiny side down. Bake in preheated oven for 12 minutes. Remove from oven; remove foil. Brush bottom of crust lightly with egg white. Return pizza to oven; bake 2 to 3 minutes. Set aside until cool, then sprinkle evenly with walnuts.

In a saucepan combine sugar, syrup and water. Bring to a boil. Lower heat; simmer 5 to 6 minutes. Add butter and stir until dissolved. Pour evenly over walnuts in crust. Return pizza to oven; bake a final 10 to 12 minutes. Cool to room temperature.

Place chocolate and butter in top half of a double boiler over simmering water. Stir until chocolate is almost melted. Remove from heat and continue to stir until smooth. Drizzle over surface of cooled pizza. Refrigerate until chocolate is firm or until ready to serve.

Serves 6 to 8.

●FRESH FRUIT TART ITALIAN-STYLE

This elegant and refreshing fresh fruit tart is especially recommended because it is easier to prepare than its French cousin, yet even more delicious.

1 egg

1 tablespoon fresh lemon juice

Pinch of salt

1½ cups unbleached all-
purpose flour

2 teaspoons sugar

¼ cup butter

1 cup ricotta cheese

¼ cup sugar

1 tablespoon Marsala wine or
sweet sherry

1 large navel orange, peeled,
cut into thick slices, each
slice cut into 4 wedges

1 pint fresh strawberries or
blueberries

In a small bowl, combine egg, lemon juice and salt. Beat with a fork.

In a large bowl, combine flour and sugar. Cut in butter with a pastry cutter or work with your fingers until you have a fine meal. With fork stir in egg mixture. Form dough into a ball, then press out into a 3″ disk and place between 2 sheets of waxed paper or plastic wrap. With fingers press out into an 8″ circle. Refrigerate about 1 hour until chilled. Without removing waxed paper or plastic wrap, roll out dough to a 14″ circle. Remove paper from one side and place, dough side down, in a 14″ pizza pan. Remove top paper and fit dough into pan. Turn overlapping dough under and up to form edging around rim of pan. Prick dough with fork at 1″ spaces and around edges of dough. Refrigerate for another 10 to 15 minutes or until ready to bake.

Preheat oven to 375° F. Bake chilled tart in preheated oven for 15 to 18 minutes or until just lightly browned. Cool to room temperature, then refrigerate until cold.

Place ricotta in a small bowl; add sugar and wine or sherry. Beat with a whisk about 5 minutes until well blended and sugar has dissolved. Refrigerate until chilled.

Spoon chilled filling into crust. Starting at center of filling, arrange orange wedges in 4 rows to edge of dough, dividing tart into 4 sections. Place strawberries or blueberries between rows of orange wedges, covering filling completely. Refrigerate tart about 1 hour or until ready to slice and serve.

Makes one 14″ tart.

●APRICOT PIZZA FLAMBÉ

Don't be hesitant about preparing this epicurean pizza. It's easy, and all but the dramatic flaming can be done ahead.

6 oz. dried apricots, chopped
2 oz. candied pineapple,
   chopped
1 cup water
1 cup sugar
2 cups flour
½ cup additional sugar
Pinch of salt
½ teaspoon cinnamon
1 cup ground almonds
1 cup butter (2 sticks) chilled,
   cut into small cubes

4 egg yolks
1 teaspoon apricot brandy
Approximately 2 teaspoons
   additional sugar
½ cup additional apricot
   brandy
¼ cup additional sugar
Vanilla ice cream or sweetened
   whipped cream (optional)

In a saucepan combine apricots, pineapple, water and sugar. Bring to a boil. Reduce heat; let simmer until liquid is reduced to about ¼ cup. Cool slightly, then purée in work bowl of food processor or blender. Set aside.

Preheat oven to 400° F.

In a large bowl combine flour, sugar, salt, cinnamon and almonds. Add chilled butter cubes. Work with fingers or pastry blender until mixture resembles coarse meal.

In small bowl beat egg yolks with brandy until well blended. Stir into flour mixture. With a fork, stir to a soft dough; form into a ball. Wrap loosely in wax paper; refrigerate until chilled.

On a floured board flatten dough to make a 6″ to 8″ circle. Place in a 12″ or 14″ pizza pan and press out evenly with fingers, covering bottom and sides of pan. With thumb and second finger flute edges to form decorative rim. Prick bottom of dough with fork in several places. Bake in preheated oven 15 to 18 minutes or until lightly browned. Place on rack and cool to room temperature. Spread with apricot mixture.

When ready to serve, place rack 3″ under broiler heat and preheat broiler to high. Sprinkle apricot filling evenly with

189

sugar and place pizza under broiler heat until sugar dissolves and bubbles.

Combine remaining sugar and brandy in small saucepan over high heat, or in chafing dish or fondue pot over high flame. Stir until sugar is dissolved and brandy begins to bubble. Ignite and pour flaming over surface of pizza. When flame dies out slice and serve—with scoops of ice cream or sweetened whipped cream, if desired.

Serves 8 to 10.

● GRANITA DI CAFFÈ
(Coffee Ice)

This sherbet-like dessert is one of the most refreshing ways to bring any meal to a close, but especially if the main course is a great, big beautiful pizza.

1 cup water	3 tablespoons coffee liqueur,
1 cup sugar	brandy or rum
1 cup freshly brewed coffee, cooled to room temperature	1 egg white

In a large, heavy saucepan, over low heat, bring water and sugar to a boil. Raise heat; boil rapidly for about 5 minutes. Cool to room temperature. Stir in coffee and liqueur. Set aside.

In a small bowl beat egg white until frothy; stir into coffee mixture.

Freeze in ice cream freezer following manufacturer's instructions. Or pour into shallow, metal pan or ice cube tray and freeze until solid around edges; then stir and crush large ice particles; refreeze and stir as before; cover and freeze until solid. Before serving, place in refrigerator for about 20 minutes to soften slightly, then quickly beat with a whisk to soften. Spoon granita into stemmed glasses or dessert bowls. Serve at once.

Makes 6 servings.

● PINK GRAPEFRUIT ICE

A ravishingly beautiful, icy cold, pale pink sherbet.

1 cup water
1 cup sugar
1 6-oz. can frozen grapefruit
  concentrate
Water

1 teaspoon grated lemon zest
2 tablespoons Grenadine syrup
Fresh mint leaves for garnish
  (optional)

Combine water and sugar in a large, heavy saucepan. Place over low heat; bring to a boil. Raise heat; let boil rapidly for about 5 minutes. Remove from heat; cool to room temperature.

Place frozen grapefruit concentrate in a 3-cup measure and let stand until mushy. Pour in enough water to make 3 cups liquid. Stir into sugar-water syrup. Stir in grated lemon zest and Grenadine syrup.

Freeze in ice cream maker, following manufacturer's instructions. Transfer frozen mixture to an airtight container and place in freezer for several hours to mellow flavors or until ready to serve.

Transfer to refrigerator to soften slightly for about 30 minutes before serving. Spoon into stemmed sherbet glasses. Garnish each serving with mint leaves, if desired.

Makes 8 to 12 servings.

● ITALIAN ORANGE AND LEMON ICE

This quickly made sherbet is an example of the icy desserts invented by the ancient Romans—they were merely frozen, slightly sweetened fruit juices. A perfect ending to a pizza meal.

1 cup water	2 teaspoons frozen lemonade
1 cup sugar	concentrate
1 tablespoon frozen orange	Water
juice concentrate	1 egg white

In a large, heavy saucepan over low heat bring water and sugar to boil. Reduce heat; boil rapidly for about 5 minutes. Remove from heat; cool to room temperature.

Place frozen orange juice and lemonade in a 1-cup measure. Let soften until mushy, then stir in water to make 1 cup. Stir into sugar water syrup. Set aside.

In a small bowl, beat egg white until frothy; stir into juice mixture.

Freeze in ice cream maker, following manufacturer's instructions. Transfer frozen mixture into an airtight container and place in freezer for several hours to develop flavors or until ready to serve. Transfer to refrigerator for about 30 minutes to soften before serving.

Serve in stemmed sherbet glasses.

Makes 6 servings.

● LIME SHERBET SURPRISE

And surprised your guests will be when they taste their first spoonful of this innocent-looking sherbet spiked with crème de menthe liqueur

1 pint lime sherbet
1 oz. crème de menthe liqueur
Whipped cream

Orange wedges or mint leaves
  for garnish

Combine sherbet and crème de menthe in an electric blender. Blend only until smooth. Pour into 6 small parfait glasses. Place in freezer until firm or until ready to serve. Top with a dollop of whipped cream and garnish with an orange wedge or mint leaf.

Makes 6 servings.

● ORANGE CHAMPAGNE GELATIN

Make this dessert the next time you want to serve something impressive. It's low calorie—no sugar is added—yet it tastes glorious, especially after a hearty main-course pizza.

2 envelopes unflavored gelatin
1/2 cup water
1 1/2 cups fresh or reconstituted
  frozen orange juice

2 cups champagne
2 navel oranges, peeled, sliced,
  slices cut into wedges

Sprinkle gelatin over 1/2 cup water in a small saucepan. Let stand until softened, about 2 minutes. Place over low heat and stir until gelatin has dissolved completely. Add orange juice and stir for about 1 minute to make sure gelatin is thoroughly mixed with juice. Remove from heat and cool to room temperature. Add champagne. Pour mixture into a medium-size bowl or decorative mold, or pour into 8 individual parfait glasses. Refrigerate until firm. Garnish with orange wedges.

Makes 8 servings.

● BISQUE TORTONI

This light but creamy, rich Italian inspiration should be served in small portions along with authentic Italian espresso spiked with a dash of anisette liqueur and a paper-thin sliver of lemon zest.

12 to 14 imported Italian amaretti or dry macaroon cookies (enough to make 1 cup crumbs)

1 pint heavy cream, chilled
2 egg whites, room temperature
1/2 cup sugar
1/3 cup dry or sweet sherry

Place amaretti cookies in work bowl of food processor or blender; process or blend to fine crumbs. (Or if using macaroon cookies, crumble each, spread out onto a long, shallow baking sheet and place in a 250° F oven until very dry and crisp before blending or processing into crumbs.)

Beat cream until soft peaks form, then beat, adding sugar a little at a time, until stiff. In a separate bowl beat egg whites until stiff peaks form; fold into beaten cream. Alternately, fold in sherry and amaretti or macaroon crumbs.

Spoon mixture into 12 paper cupcake liners in muffin tins. Cover muffin tins with foil. Place in freezer until tortoni are firm or until ready to serve.

Makes 12 individual servings.

Note: If desired, tortoni can be spooned into one loaf pan and frozen as above. To serve, dip pan briefly in warm water, turn tortoni out onto serving platter and cut into slices.

● ICE CREAM AMBROSIA

We've always said that no one could improve on old-fashioned vanilla ice cream or on Southern ambrosia, but now we take it all back. This elegant recipe is just fabulous. And so easy to make!

1 pint vanilla ice cream   8 tablespoons crème de menthe
1 cup flaked coconut   liqueur or Grenadine syrup

Let ice cream stand at room temperature until slightly softened. Form into 4 balls. Roll each in flaked coconut. Place, so they are not touching each other, in freezer until very firm or until ready to serve. Then place each in a serving bowl. Pour about 2 tablespoons crème de menthe or Grenadine syrup over each serving. Serve at once.

Makes 4 servings.

● BRANDIED APPLES

Serve these tipsy apple slices over vanilla ice cream.

4 crisp tart apples, peeled,   ½ cup brown sugar
  cored and chopped   ¼ teaspoon powdered ginger
6 tablespoons butter   ¼ cup brandy

Melt butter in a skillet. Stir in sugar and ginger. Add chopped apples and cook over medium heat, stirring occasionally to prevent sticking, about 5 minutes. When apples are crisp-tender, stir in brandy and cook another minute.

Makes topping for 6 to 8 servings of ice cream.

Appendix: Some Sources for Ordering by Mail

Italian groceries: semolina (durum wheat flour), fine fresh olive oil, imported cheeses, sausages, Italian delicacies such as sun-dried tomatoes packed in oil, etc.

New York

Manganaro Foods
488 9th Avenue
New York, New York 10018

Todaro Brothers
555 2nd Avenue
New York, New York 10016

Midwest

LL Conte Di Savoia
555 West Roosevelt Road
Chicago, Illinois 60607

Riviera Italian Foods
3220 North Harlem Avenue
Harwood Heights, Illinois
     60656

Other sources for semolina

Paprikas Weiss
1546 2nd Avenue
New York, New York 10021

El Molino Mills
345 North Baldwin Park
    Boulevard
Industry, California 91746

Pizza pans, baking stones, baker's peels and other pizza-making equipment

Sassafras Enterprises, Inc.
Post Office Box 1366
Evanston, Illinois 60204

Williams-Sonoma
Post Office Box 7456
San Francisco, California
    94120

Housewares Division
Fowley Manufacturing Com-
    pany
3300 Northeast 5th Street
Minneapolis, Minnesota
    55418

Index